Jo-Anne Elikann

111 Places in New York That You Must Not Miss

Edited by Susan Lusk

emons:

Bibliographical Information of the Deutsche Nationalbibliothek
The Deutsche Nationalbibliothek lists this publication
in the Deutsche Nationalbibliografie; detailed bibliographical
data are available on the internet at http://dnb.d-nb.de

© Emons Verlag GmbH
All rights reserved
Design: TIZIAN BOOKS, based on a design
by Lübbekke / Naumann / Thoben
German editor: Monika Elisa Schurr
Copy editor: Mark Gabor
Typesetting and digital processing: Gerd Wiechcinski
Maps / Cartography: altancicek.design, www.altancicek.de
Maps based on data by Openstreetmap, © Openstreet Map-participants, ODbL
Printing and binding: B.O.S.S Medien GmbH, Goch
Printed in Germany 2016
ISBN 978-3-95451-052-8
Revised third edition, September 2016

Did you enjoy it? Do you want more?
Join us in uncovering new places around the world on:
www.111places.com

Foreword

For over twenty years, I played a fascinating game with New York and myself. On Saturdays and Sundays I ventured into neighborhoods I didn't know and became an adventurous tourist eager to explore parts of a city I'd never visited before.

I rode there by subway or bus, strolled through streets and parks, poked my head into shops, galleries, houses of worship, and little cafes. Stopping for coffee and a sandwich at a busy diner or a burger and beer in a tavern, I'd strike up a conversation with locals to learn as much as I could about the area. When someone mentioned a special place known mostly to neighborhood folks, I made a beeline there. Back home, along with tired feet, I'd have a whole bunch of photos and a headful of new experiences and stories to share with friends and family.

I never imagined I'd have an opportunity to author a book on these out-of-the-way places, little-known aspects of well-known landmarks, and assorted unusual spots I had discovered on my weekend explorations. But true to the city's reputation as a place of infinite possibility, I was asked (quite unexpectedly!) to create this book and introduce a world of visitors – as well as my fellow New Yorkers – to 111 not-to-be-missed places that you just don't find in other travel guides.

I accepted the challenge with great enthusiasm and spent more than a year revisiting some old gems and uncovering many new ones – and photographing a thrilling assortment of truly remarkable must-see destinations. Throughout this process, I've had the great good fortune to get acquainted with artists, historians, proprietors, tradespeople, curators, journalists, and adventurous New Yorkers of every description – exceptional women and men who've welcomed and enlightened me, often providing valuable insights and inside stories to enrich my experience and add juice to my text.

With reverence and delight, I happily present this, my love letter to New York City.

111 Places

1__ The Afro Archives

Black gold on Malcolm X Boulevard

It's the most prestigious research library in the United States that focuses on African Americans, the African Diaspora, and the African experience, with about ten million items in its several collections. If you expect this venerable institution to be intimidating or stuffy, you're in for a surprise.

Doors to The Schomburg Center open on a contemporary space. A genial staff is eager to assist – whether you're a scholar of Harlem Renaissance art, a student writing an essay on Marcus Garvey, a Motown enthusiast, or a curious visitor. Galleries, reading rooms, and research resources are open to all. The more you explore, the more astonished you'll be at the treasures you have access to.

In 1926, the collection of African-American material belonging to black Puerto Rican scholar Arturo Schomburg was donated to a Harlem branch library, and named the Division of Negro Literature, History, and Prints. As its research reputation grew, other significant local, national, and international African-American collections were added. It was designated one of the NY Public Library's four main research libraries in 1972, renamed to honor its original donor, and moved to its present site in 1980.

Five remarkable sub-collections – Research & Reference; Manuscript, Archives & Rare Books; Art & Artifacts; Photographs & Prints; and Moving Image & Recorded Sound – enable you to read the original manuscript of Richard Wright's *Native Son*, preserved slave diaries, and congressional records. You can view art from Benin to Brooklyn, hear the voice of Malcolm X or Etta James, or read a Kenyan newspaper from your ergonomically-designed reading room chair.

It's also a vibrant community center. With museum-worthy changing exhibits on thought-provoking (and fun) themes and talks, workshops, performances, screenings, and social gatherings for young and old, Schomburg's is an uptown goldmine.

Address 515 Malcolm X Boulevard (between West 135th and 136th Street),
New York 10037, Phone +1 212.491.2200, www.schomburgcenter.org | Transit Subway:
135 St (2, 3), Bus: M 1, M 2, M 7, M 102 | Hours Mon 10am – 6pm, Tue –Thu 10am – 8pm,
Fri – Sat 10am – 6pm, closed Sun | Tip Across the street, Harlem Hospital's Mural Pavilion
displays restored murals historically depicting the life and work of black people. Painted
in 1936, they were the first Works Progress Administration (WPA) commission for black
artists in the US.

2 The Algonquin Lounge
Legendary literary lair

For years the lobby lounge of the Algonquin Hotel has been the quintessential spot for a *soigné* midtown rendezvous. Whatever the hour, lights are low and it's cocktail time. Despite its spaciousness, the elegant room's tasteful placement of upholstered settees, armchairs, and softly shaded lamps encourages comfortable, even intimate, conversation. Beneath potted palms and tall mahogany columns, tucked-away corners offer privacy for discreet *tête-à-têtes*.

Conversation is what the Algonquin is most famous for. In the 1920s it's where that infamous group of about a dozen sharp-tongued, witty writers and theater people met for lunch every day for nearly a decade to trade ideas, banter, gossip, and generally outdo one another's clever quips. They called themselves the Vicious Circle. But when a *Brooklyn Eagle* editorial cartoonist caricatured them clad in suits of armor and redubbed them the Round Table, it stuck. This mutual admiration society was the cream of New York's literati: critics, columnists, playwrights, and authors, whose charter members included Dorothy Parker, Robert Benchley, George S. Kaufman, Alexander Woollcott, and *New Yorker* magazine founder Harold Ross. A colorful mural in the lobby immortalizes the group, and these celebrated ghosts remain in residence to this day.

Though major renovations and updates have been made by various owners since the hotel opened its doors in 1902, the lounge's unique character endures. Wifi throughout encourages the *bon mots* of bloggers and tweeters, today's online quipsters. The location, steps away from Broadway theaters, is a perfect place to meet a companion before a show or nurse a nightcap after. Immerse yourselves in old-world ambiance and sip the signature Algonquin Cocktail: rye whiskey, dry vermouth, and pineapple juice. Order a Dorothy Parker mini-burger from the bar menu — she surely would have had a good laugh at that.

Address 59 West 44th Street (between Fifth Avenue and Avenue of the Americas), New York 10036, Phone +1 212.840.6800, www.algonquinhotel.com | **Transit** Subway: 42 St-Bryant Pk (B, D, F, M); Grand Central-42 St (4, 5, 6, S); Times Sq-42 St (1, 2, 3, N, Q, R), Bus: M 1, M 2, M 3, M 4, M 5, M 7, M 20, M 42 | **Tip** Nearby, same-day discount theater tickets (up to 50% off) for many shows are available at the Times Square TKTS booth.

3 _ Alice Austen House

Photographic memory

Wealthy nineteenth-century New Yorkers made their summer homes on Staten Island's shore. Alice Austen's house, Clear Comfort, overlooked NY Harbor, the Statue of Liberty, and lower Manhattan. She was one of the earliest and most prolific female photographers in the US.

Alice was two in 1868 when her father left and she and her mother moved to this, her grandparents' home. When she was ten, a sea-captain uncle let her tinker with a camera acquired on his travels. It was a large intricate device with heavy glass plates, but she learned to master it. She took 8,000 pictures in her lifetime. Some were staged, depicting family and friends at play (sailing, yachting, riding) with Alice herself in the frame, shutter-release in hand. Or she'd haul the cumbersome camera onto the ferry to explore Manhattan's dim corners, documenting lives of the poor, displaced, and diseased.

An ace tennis player, cyclist, and the first Staten Island woman to own a car, Alice bucked convention, spent her days in the company of women, and for fifty years lived with her friend Gertrude Tate. When the 1929 stock market crash left her a pauper, she mortgaged the house, sold its contents, and eventually ended up in a county poorhouse. In 1951, 3,000 of her photo plates were found in a storage area of the Staten Island Historical Society, and Alice's artistry was celebrated. She was transferred to a private nursing home and, before she died, attended a gala reception held in her honor at Clear Comfort.

In recent years her Victorian Gothic cottage was lovingly restored – the parlor is recaptured as it appeared in its heyday, displaying a camera like Alice's. Hallways are lined with her work. There's a gallery for contemporary exhibits, a film about her, and a library. Come to picnic on the lawn, attend its cultural programs and activities, and celebrate the art of photography and a woman of independent spirit.

Address 2 Hylan Boulevard (at Edgewater Street), Staten Island, New York 10305, Phone +1 718.816.4506, www.aliceausten.org, info@aliceausten.org | Transit to Staten Island Ferry: Subway: South Ferry (1); Bowling Green (4, 5); Whitehall St-South Ferry (R), Bus: M5, M15, M20; from ferry terminal in Staten Island: Bus: S51 (to Hylan Boulevard) | Hours Mar.–Dec. Tue–Sun 11am–5pm; Jan., Feb. by appointment | Tip Visit a quirky gallery behind the counter at DeLuca General Store on Bay Street, where folk-art lovers go wild over robots, battleships, planes, and rockets Mr. DeLuca made from found objects.

4__Artists of Color

A treasure trove in the heart of Harlem

An exciting and compelling art museum is smack-dab in the middle of Harlem's main thoroughfare, the bustling shopping and entertainment concourse that is 125th Street. The Studio Museum in Harlem is a bright, airy, three-story contemporary showplace that thrives on the dynamic energy of this boulevard while providing a refuge from its noise and commotion.

When you visit, thrill to a wonderful display of important art by both established and little-known African-American artists, from the nineteenth century to the present day. The museum's permanent collection and temporary exhibits present an exceptionally diverse assemblage of paintings, photographs, sculpture, textile art, masks, and mixed media. Works by Romare Bearden and Jacob Lawrence creatively interact with Carrie Mae Weems' photographs and installations by label-defying new artists. Contrasts and similarities reverberate and the results are stunning.

At first, everything in the gallery looks beautiful. As you take a closer look, powerful themes of the American black experience emerge. You'll discover works that expose, prod, and often break boundaries of race, color, and gender. Other examples portray historical narratives or current hot-button issues.

Art's power to transform is central to the museum's philosophy. Founded in 1968, the Studio Museum was the first institution in the US dedicated entirely to artists of African descent. Its founders' desire to make this cultural experience accessible to the community was fulfilled in 1977 when it relocated from a rented loft to its present street-level location.

For over forty years, the artist-in-residence program has provided studio space to foster the careers of emerging talents. Innovative educational programs for schoolchildren and teachers, lectures, discussions, and performances bring art to life for Harlem neighbors as well as visitors from communities around the world.

Address 144 West 125th Street (between Malcolm X and Adam Clayton Powell Jr. Boulevard), New York 10027, Phone +1 212.864.4500, www.studiomuseum.org, info@studiomusuem.org | **Transit** Subway: 125 St (A, B, C, D, 2, 3, 4, 5, 6), Bus: M 1, M 2, M 3, M 7, M 10, M 60, M 100, M 101, M 102 | **Hours** Thu – Fri noon – 9pm, Sat 10am – 6pm, Sun noon – 6pm | **Tip** Blackened catfish is a crowd-pleaser at celebrity chef Marcus Samuelsson's Red Rooster Harlem on Malcolm X Boulevard.

5__B&H Dairy Restaurant

Comfort food from the old country

Lower Second Avenue was once known as the Yiddish Broadway, a vibrant entertainment hub for crowds of Eastern European Jewish immigrants living in tenements and brownstones in what is today's East Village. Theaters and vaudeville houses lined the bustling sidewalks alongside restaurants featuring huge servings of traditional dishes, tastes of the 'old country,' just like *bubbe* (grandma) used to make. Kosher dietary law prohibits combining meat and milk products, so some eateries served meals containing meat while others, like B&H, offered meatless dishes familiarly called 'dairy.'

Time-worn and tiny, its aisle is so narrow between the counter stools and six small tables that even skinny-minnies making their way to a rear table risk jostling somebody's *pierogies*. Original owner Abie Bergson (the B of B&H) had no desire to expand the cramped dining area, insisting it was far better to have customers waiting for tables than tables waiting for customers. Staying small may be one reason why it's been going strong since 1938, while larger rivals (like Ratner's and Rappaport's) have since closed their doors.

The staff is mainly Hispanic now, yet old-timers claim the menu of Jewish soul food hasn't changed since opening day. Heaping plates ('Is all of this for me?') of *blintzes, latkes, kasha varnishkas*, and bowls of lentil, split pea, hot or cold *borscht*, and veggie matzoball soup come with house-baked buttered *challah* bread – the basis for what many deem NY's best French toast and grilled cheese sandwiches. Sip an egg cream or fresh-pressed fruit juice. Signs on the wall list menu items, daily soups and specials – and all at surprisingly gentle prices.

Over the years, B&H has fed hungry actors, beatniks, hippies, hipsters, college kids, and hard-core regulars. If you're lucky, you'll be elbow-to-elbow at the counter with an octogenarian who'll bend your ear about great food and the good old days.

Address 127 Second Avenue (between East 7th Street and St Marks Place), New York 10003, Phone +1 212.505.8065 | **Transit** Subway: Astor Pl (6); 8 St-NYU (N, R), Bus: M 1, M 2, M 3, M 8, M 15, M 101, M 102, M 103 | **Hours** Sun–Thu 7am–11pm, Fri–Sat 7am–midnight | **Tip** Jewish old-world bakery treats like *babka*, *rugelach*, and fruit-filled *hamantaschen* fill the shelves nearby at Moishe's Bake Shop.

6_ The Back Room
Tabooze in a teacup

This could be the only bar whose bouncer directs you to the door. "The Back Room? … down here!" He points to a metal gate with a *Lower East Side Toy Company* sign. Stairs take you down to a grim-looking alley. Rusty iron steps at the far end lead to a closed door. Be brave, go inside. It's dimly lit but sparkly. Smiling, attractive people cluster and dance beside a roaring-twenties mirrored bar running along the front wall. Paintings of saucy ladies leer provocatively from the sidelines. Up some carpeted steps, a posh lounge oozes with period decor – red velvet settees, cocktail tables, and *objets d'art* elegantly arranged in the warm glow of a fireplace and twinkling chandeliers. With a nod to the days when booze was outlawed and consumed in secret, the Back Room's potent cocktails are served 'disguised' in teacups, bottle beer in brown paper bags, drafts in coffee mugs, and shots in espresso cups.

Various trendy bars in the city pretend to be speakeasies. But this tucked-away night spot is the real deal – an authentic, clandestine drinking lounge that flourished during Prohibition. Back then you entered through the rear door of Ratner's, a famous Lower East Side dairy restaurant. Open round the clock, Ratner's *blintzes* and fresh-baked onion rolls drew all-night crowds that included Al Jolson, Fanny Brice, and Groucho Marx, along with notorious gangsters like Bugsy Siegel, Lucky Luciano, and Meyer Lansky. After eating kosher delicacies they'd sneak into *the back room* for booze. Celebrities are still spotted here. Pearl Jam presided over the club's 2005 reopening party; star-power patrons reserve bottle-service-only tables or throw lavish parties in its hidden Back Of The Back Room room.

Toast the twenties into the wee hours. Weekends are wild. Live jazz at Lucky's Lounge Mondays requires a password at the door, and Poetry Brothels on the last Sunday of the month defy polite description.

Address 102 Norfolk Street (between Delancey and Rivington Street), New York 10002, Phone +1 212.228.5098, www.backroomnyc.com, info@backroomnyc.com | **Transit** Subway: Essex St (J, M, Z); Delancey St (F); Grand St (B, D), Bus: M 9, M 14, M 15, M 21 | **Hours** Sun – Mon 7:30pm – 2am, Tue –Thu 7:30pm – 3am, Fri – Sat 7:30pm – 4am | **Tip** If you work up a hunger dancing, Schiller's on Rivington serves late suppers until 3am on Fridays and Saturdays.

7 __ The Batman-Poe Connection

Partners in crime?

Edgar Allan Poe was a master of the modern detective story. Batman is a master sleuth. It may sound crazy to suggest a link between a nineteenth-century literary giant and a twentieth-century comics superhero, but there's a park on the Bronx's Grand Concourse where these two 'lives' actually do intersect.

In 1846, hoping the fresh air of the then-rural Bronx would prove beneficial to his tubercular wife Virginia, Poe rented a small wood-frame cottage for $100/year and moved there with her and her mother. After a year of living humbly but happily, Virginia died. Poe remained there (writing *The Bells* and *Annabel Lee* in one of the rooms) until his death in 1849.

Over the years, the Grand Concourse became a busy residential boulevard. In 1913, tiny Poe Cottage was relocated to a park across the street, later named in the poet's honor. Docents provide guided tours through the cozy house. Sparsely furnished, some original pieces remain – like a scuffed mirror and the bed where his beloved Virginia died. A Visitor Center was built, its design echoing the wingspan of a raven (after Poe's most famous poem), with roof tiles resembling dark feathers. Poe's fans come from all over the world to see where he lived and wrote, while locals take their kids to the playground and attend seasonal events at the 1925-vintage bandstand.

A little-known factoid is what unites our two heroes: in 1939, neighborhood pals Bob Kane and Bill Finger sat on a Poe Park bench and hatched the idea for Batman. They met here regularly to brainstorm details of the new comic strip, trying to rival the recent success of Superman. Together they dreamed up costumes and storylines for Batman, his sidekick Robin, and their diabolical arch-villains. It's no riddle, then, why many of the caped crusader's thrilling escapades were inspired by tales penned by Edgar Allan Poe.

Address Poe Cottage: 194th Street and Kingsbridge Road, Bronx, New York 10458; Poe Park Visitor Center: 2640 Grand Concourse, Bronx, New York 10458, Phone +1 718.365.5516 | **Transit** Subway: Kingsbridge Rd (B, D, 4), Bus: BX 1, BX 2, BX 9, BX 12, BX 22, BX 28, BX 32, BX 34 | **Hours** Poe Park: daily 7am–10pm; Visitor Center: Tue–Sat 8am–4pm; Poe Cottage: Thu–Fri 10am–3pm, Sat 10am–4pm, Sun 1pm–5pm | **Tip** As a boy, director Stanley Kubrick lived nearby and thrilled to movies at palatial Loew's Paradise Theater (188th Street & Grand Concourse).

8___Berlin Wall Remnants
The art of freedom

For more than twenty years, an imposing 12-foot-high and 20-foot-long section of the graffiti-covered Berlin Wall stood outdoors (shown opposite) flanked by vertical waterfalls in a compact urban space called a "pocket park." Relaxing among the sitting areas tucked in between towering office buildings, workers who spent their lunch breaks there hardly took notice of the colorful monoliths. In 2015, following an extensive conservation and restoration project to preserve these stunning witnesses to history, they were relocated just steps away, inside the elegant marble-clad 53rd Street entrance lobby of 520 Madison Avenue.

The striking images on display were painted between 1984 and 1985 by Thierry Noir, an artist who lived in an apartment along the Waldemarstrasse in Berlin Kreuzberg, adjacent to a section of the Berlin Wall. With the assistance of fellow artists Christophe Bouchet, Kiddy Citny, and other revolutionary friends, Noir sought to use paint to transform the imposing, fearsome wall into colorful cartoon-like images, to render it less threatening and, ultimately, to help destroy it. By the time the wall came down in 1989, they had painted a length of nearly five kilometers on the West Berlin side of the wall. Their vivid and provocative images came to symbolize liberation and freedom throughout Germany.

In 1990, when pieces of the wall were sold at auction in Europe, Jerry Speyer, president of the American real estate company Tishman Speyer, purchased these five remnants and arranged to have them brought to New York. Speyer celebrated the demise of communism in Germany by situating his treasured portion of the Berlin Wall in the home of American capitalism. In a rather interesting sidelight, German director Wim Wenders' iconic film, *Wings of Desire*, features a scene in which Thierry Noir is painting these exact images of freedom on the wall.

Address 520 Madison Avenue (East 53rd Street between Fifth Avenue and Madison Avenue), New York 10022 | Transit Subway: 5 Av-53 St (E, M); 51 St (6), Bus: M1, M2, M3, M4, M50, M101, M103 | Hours Daily 24 hours | Tip Other Berlin Wall segments in NYC: at the entrance of the Intrepid Sea-Air-Space Museum; between Gateway Plaza and World Financial Center; in the garden area of United Nations headquarters.

9 Bloomingdale's Retro Restroom

Powder your nose in a Deco ladies' lounge

When you're on the go and need to *go*, finding a nearby restroom can be a challenge. Savvy cityfolk keep a personal mental inventory of clean, attractive, readily accessible bathrooms. But for visitors, the prospect of locating and availing themselves of a public toilet is cringeworthy, evoking images that are anything but glamorous. Like any major metropolis, NYC has its share of unsavory restrooms, but when you know where to look, you'll find a wealth of great places to go for relief.

Department stores, Barnes & Noble bookshops, Apple stores, Whole Foods Markets, Rockefeller Center, and Time Warner Center all have pleasant public washrooms. The lobbies of posh hotels have excellent ones – simply waltz in and pretend you're a guest. And in Greenwich Village, you don't need to buy a movie ticket to pay a visit to the bathrooms at the Angelica Theater's cafe.

Ladies looking for a lovely loo in midtown make a beeline to the fourth-floor women's lounge in Bloomingdale's, where the facilities are positively gorgeous.

It's decked out in Art Deco-style glamour – gleaming white and black marble floors, silver-gray walls, black-granite countertops, chrome sconces shaded with white linen, and beveled illuminated mirrors. To make shoppers feel pretty, the ambience is designed to flatter. Inside its entrance is an elegant lounge to rest tired feet, and a bank of vanity tables for urban divas to refresh their makeup. The wash-up area's long double row of porcelain basins have individual mirrors, lighting, towels, and delicate-scented liquid hand soap. Small vestibules lead to private *toilettes* behind frosted-glass doors.

In this ultra-chic setting, you may be tempted to linger, relax, and freshen up. On your way out – your comfort restored – perhaps you might even browse the latest fashions.

Isn't it simply de-lovely?!

Address Bloomingdale's, 1000 Third Avenue (between East 59th and 60th Street) New York 10022, Phone +1 212.705.2000 | Transit Subway: Lexington Av-59 St (4, 5, 6, N, Q, R); Lexington Av-63 St (F); Lexington Av-53 St (E, M), Bus: M1, M3, M4, M15, M31, M57, M101, M102, M103 | Hours Mon–Fri 10am–8:30pm, Sat 10am–7pm, Sun 11am–7pm | Tip Men deserve pampering too: The Art of Shaving (141 East 62nd Street) is a thoroughly masculine emporium for fine shaving and grooming accessories.

10 Bocce at Il Vagabondo
Dinner rolls

In the early 1900s, proprietor Ernest Vogliano's grandfather founded Il Vagabondo and built in a bocce court to attract this Upper East Side neighborhood's Italian immigrants, who enjoyed playing the game and hanging out with friends. As a local gathering place for espresso and bocce, its popularity soared when alcohol, sandwiches, and spaghetti were served. In 1965, record crowds flocked to the restaurant to enjoy an expanded menu of authentic Italian dishes, as well as the novelty of its bocce court, and soon two adjacent townhouses were annexed to accommodate the overflow.

The bar up front is known for old-world ambiance and a congenial vibe. A doorway to the back room leads to a bustling dining room on the left side and the indoor bocce court on the right. The court is narrower in size than regulation outdoor courts, and its surface is clay. The wooden balls are rolled instead of thrown, to prevent them from flying up and clobbering nearby diners. In place of the traditional small target-ball called a *pallino*, the target here is a large metal ring. Two players at a time compete, taking turns to roll four balls each (one player's set is green, the other's red) toward the target. When all balls are rolled, the round ends, and the player whose ball is closest to the target scores a point. The first to score eleven points is the winner.

It's fun to watch the competition from a courtside table, sipping wine and savoring scrumptious Italian cuisine. Visiting celebrity chef Emeril Lagasse claims that Il Vagabondo's veal parmigiana is the best in the world. And for dessert, order a 'bocce ball' – a sphere of ice cream covered with a layer of dark chocolate. No playing is allowed while you're dining, but before or after, you're encouraged to give it a whirl. You might just run into celebs like Cindy Crawford and Tom Hanks, who've been spotted on the court just letting the good times roll.

Address 351 East 62nd Street (between First and Second Avenue), New York 10021, Phone +1 212.832.9221, www.ilvagabondo.com, bocce@ilvagabondo.com | Transit Subway: Lexington Av-59 St (4, 5, 6, N, R); Lexington Av-63 St (F), Bus: M 15, M 31, M 57, M 66, M 101, M 102, M 103 | Hours Mon – Fri noon – 3pm, 5:30 –11pm, Sat 5:30 –11:30pm, Sun 5:30 –11pm | Tip Laugh it up around the corner at Dangerfield's, NY's longest-running comedy club, with its nightly line-up of hilarious comics.

11__Bohemian National Hall
Reality Czech

One of the city's many exciting venues for contemporary art, music, film, and theater is this little-known treasure on a sleepy Upper East Side street. Judging by its exterior, Bohemian National Hall is an elegant neo-Renaissance townhouse. But step inside for a postmodern surprise: a sleek white-on-white lobby emblazoned with catchphrases and quotes, multimedia screen projections, and a glassed-in art gallery. The bright yellow reception desk faces a space-age spiral staircase and state-of-the-art screening room.

Various local and international organizations within Bohemian National Hall are dedicated to promoting and celebrating Czech culture in the United States, encouraging dynamic dialogue between American and Czech communities, and presenting a richly diverse calendar of events. It's filled with free performances, exhibits, rooftop screenings, lectures, workshops, and galas – all presented (or subtitled) in English. There's something for everyone, including Hospoda, a sophisticated gastropub with an inventive menu and pilsner pumped four distinct ways.

Originally built in 1897 by local Czech and Slovak immigrants as a social hall, it was central to community life – with a theater, ballroom, club rooms, gymnasium, bowling alley, even a rifle range. For nearly a century it played an essential role in the neighborhood by providing a place for gatherings, special events, language education, political action, and the exchange of ideas. But as the area's Czech population dwindled, the building fell into disrepair. In 2001, ownership was transferred to the Czech Republic for one dollar, and renovation began. By 2008 the major overhaul, incorporating restoration with dramatic interior re-design, was complete. The revived Bohemian National Hall – now also home to the Consulate General of the Czech Republic – has become a vibrant cultural venue for new generations of New Yorkers.

Address 321 East 73rd Street (between First and Second Avenue), New York 10021, Phone +1 212.988.1733, www.bohemiannationalhall.com, www.czechcenter.com | Transit Subway: 77 St (6), Bus: M 15, M 68, M 72, M 79, M 101, M 102, M 103 | Hours Daily 10am–6pm | Tip View (and bid on) fine art and antiques on exhibit at Sotheby's, the legendary international auction house, 72nd Street & York Avenue.

12 __ Brooklyn Boulders

Have the climb of your life

There's no big sign outside announcing the entrance to Brooklyn Boulders, so look hard to find the unobtrusive, graffiti-lettered door that's the portal to a color-blasted, irresistible paradise for climbers, daredevils, and those who aspire to great heights.

It's a sensational purple, aqua, green, blue, and pink playground. And it's huge! 22,000 square feet, the largest climbing gym in NYC! Walls, ceilings, and rooms twist, turn, and soar skyward above thick, foam-cushioned floors. The centerpiece is a giant replica of a Brooklyn Bridge tower, its tall arches enticing wannabe Spidermen/women/girls/boys.

Thrill-seeking climbers of all ages, sizes, and skills ascend and dangle on high. Sign the requisite liability waiver, and get started. Climbing surfaces have color-coded grips with tapes that mark each route and indicate its level of difficulty. Harnesses and shoes can be rented.

There are three types of activities. *Bouldering* – climbing on relatively low walls without ropes – is open to all. In *top roping* one end of a rope is attached to your harness, the other runs through an anchor at the top of the route, then down to a *belayer* – a staffer on the ground who controls the rope. You must be certified for this type of climb before you can participate. *Lead climbing* – the most advanced and challenging form of roped climbing – requires certification by head instructors. Classes for all levels are offered.

Brooklyn Boulders opened in 2009. Their motto, *Climbing + Community*, applies to their inventive school programs, team competitions, special events, and a foundation benefiting urban youth. Fabulous painted murals, adorning every non-climbing surface, are the work of NYC street artists.

Expert staff is always on hand to assist and cheer you on. The music's great, your workout is intense. Bring a date, throw a party, or find new friends – this is a place where you'll rise to the top.

Address 575 Degraw Street (between 3rd and 4th Avenue), Brooklyn, New York 11217, Phone +1 347.834.9066, www.brooklynboulders.com, info@brooklynboulders.com | Transit Subway: Union St (R), Bus: B 37, B 63, B 103 | Hours Mon, Wed and Fri – Sun 8am – midnight, Tue and Thu 7am – midnight | Tip After your workout, head to Pickle Shack on 4th Avenue for homemade artisanal pickles, craft beer, and locally sourced edible delights.

13 _ Bubble Building

Downtown's newest 'architecture row'

Innovative architecture has performed a radical make-over to the crumbling industrial waterfront of Manhattan's Meatpacking District. This former stretch of abandoned factories, warehouses, and garages has been transformed into a chic gold coast with a hip new personality.

Exceptionally eye-catching is IAC (InterActiveCorp) headquarters. Glimpsed from a distance for the first time – from the High Line or the Hudson River bike path or highway – it inspires a *wow* moment. Viewed from below 18th Street it's softly kinetic, like a tiered beehive or improbably angular, milky-white soap bubbles. Seen from 19th Street and north, its profile is dynamic and crisp, like the billowing sails of tall ships or folds of a giant pleated skirt. Its structural character changes as you walk around it.

Fans of contemporary architecture will recognize the work of Frank Gehry. It's his first New York building, and while his preliminary plan envisioned a titanium facade – one of Gehry's signature elements – IAC's chairman (media and internet mogul Barry Diller) mandated a smooth, curving *glass* exterior. While sheets of steel or titanium could be factory-shaped prior to installation, thick glass panels could not. Gehry's revised design met this challenge, and the glass was bent ("cold warped") on-site during construction. The building's 'puffy' form creates a variety of unusual interior layouts. Its enormous lobby has one of the world's largest high-resolution video walls, morphing abstract color compositions at highway level.

A stroll through this vibrant area reveals IAC's residential neighbors, Jean Nouvel's curved mosaic-like building of sharp-edged, colored-glass panels; Richard Meier's see-thru towers; artist Julian Schnabel's pink *palazzo* built atop a former stable; and the Whitney Museum's new home. New York has always embraced creative change, and this architectural parade sure struts its stuff.

Address 555 West 18th Street (at Eleventh Avenue), New York 10011 |
Transit Subway: 23 St (1, C, E), Bus: M 11, M 12, M 14D, M 23 | Tip Westbeth
(55 Bethune Street) is one of the first examples of old industrial buildings repurposed
as affordable housing for artists. Opened in 1970, it's a complex of residences, studios,
galleries, and performance spaces.

14__Building 92

The Navy Yard goes green

It's in a gritty neighborhood with a housing project, commercial buildings, and a NYPD towed-vehicle lot. In its early days as a naval base surrounded by brothels and gambling houses, Brooklyn Navy Yard's three hundred waterfront acres were sealed off by barbed-wire walls plastered with *Keep Out* signs. Today its gates are flung open and the repurposed Yard is a hugely successful engine of job creation and urban industrial growth, spurring a manufacturing revival in New York City.

So monumental in scale, the site is almost too much to take in. Building 92 comes to the rescue. It's the Yard's welcome mat, a launch pad for bus and bike tours (bring your own or rent a CitiBike), and home to must-see interactive exhibits on its maritime and wartime past (battleship *USS Arizona*, sunk at Pearl Harbor, was built here), its innovative present, and visionary future. The free employment center is a hiring boon to the Yard's businesses and area residents, who make up a quarter of the workforce.

Today's Navy Yard functions entirely off the grid – self-sufficient with its own power, trash removal/recycling, and security force. Green and sustainable technology prevails. During the devastating Hurricane Sandy of 2012, the solar/wind-powered street lamps developed by one of its industrial tenants stayed lit when other streetlight systems failed.

Manufacturers, entrepreneurs, artisans, and artists work in the Yard's forty buildings, from a vintage eighteenth-century machine shop to state-of-the-art all-green construction. Among its diverse tenants: the biggest rooftop farm in the US; a vast film studio complex; makers of military body armor; the first NYC whiskey distillery since Prohibition; the set design studio for *Saturday Night Live*. Maintenance facilities for ships, tugs, ferries and barges are provided at its massive dry docks – one so huge it could fit the entire Empire State Building lying on its side!

Address 63 Flushing Avenue (between Oxford and Cumberland Street), Brooklyn, New York 11205, Phone +1 718.907.5992, www.bldg92.org, info@bldg92.org | Transit Subway: High St (A, C); York St (F); Clinton-Washington Av (G), Bus: B 48, B 57, B 62, B 67, B 69 | Hours Wed–Sun noon–6pm | Tip Taste moonshine on the Whiskey Wars Tour at Kings County Distillery and discover the wild history of Brooklyn booze-making.

15__CBGB's Fashion Makeover

From punk hall to posh haberdashery

The Ramones played their first gig at CBGB. The down-and-dirty cave on then-seedy Bowery – stinking of cigarettes, stale beer, sweat (and don't ask what else) – was the cradle of American punk, art rock, and new wave. Hilly Kristal opened it in 1973 and named it to reflect the music he expected to feature. CBGB OMFUG stood for *Country Blue Grass and Blues – Other Music For Uplifting Gormandizers*, but after punk bands invaded, nastier versions of the acronym were invented.

Rockers from all over came to hear Talking Heads, Joan Jett & the Blackhearts, Blondie, Patti Smith, the B-52s, Guns N' Roses, Korn – artists of the seventies, eighties, and nineties who defined the era's wildest, edgiest sounds. It was a raw, tough, often ugly scene. After years of rent disputes with his landlord, Hilly gave it up. When their lease expired in October 2006, Patti Smith played a final show, and CBGB shut its doors forever.

The following year, fashion designer John Varvatos was scouting a downtown address for his ultra-cool men's boutique and heard that a bank was about to take over – and demolish – CBGB. A Detroit boy and a rocker at heart, Varvatos not only rescued it from the wrecking ball, he turned it into an upscale shop/museum – preserving the club's gritty bones as a backdrop to pricey classic menswear with rock roots.

Buttery-soft leather jackets and boots are artfully arranged by blistering walls plastered with the punk club's original graffiti and ephemera: stickers, tickets, flyers, posters. A rack of posh cashmeres hangs near the tunnel leading to what was the club's grubby toilet. Rock memorabilia, vintage vinyl, books, and photos are displayed for sale beneath the shop's lavish chandelier.

Ringo has appeared in Varvatos ads. The boutique doubles as a concert venue and there's no telling which rock legend might appear at one of the monthly Bowery Live shows. The ghost of CBGB lives!

Address 315 Bowery (at Bleecker Street), New York 10003, Phone +1 212.358.0315, www.johnvarvatos.com | **Transit** Subway: Bleecker St (6); 2 Av (F); Broadway-Lafayette St (B, D, M); Bowery (J); Prince St (N, R), Bus: M1, M2, M3, M8, M9, M15, M21, M101, M102, M103 | **Hours** Mon–Fri noon–8pm, Sat 11am–8pm, Sun noon–6pm | **Tip** House-made sausage is the one of the stars at chef Daniel Boulud's DBGB Kitchen & Bar (299 Bowery), named in honor of CBGB.

16___Chaim Gross's Village Studio

The way to a man's art

Towering sculptural figures writhe, dance, and mingle inside renowned artist Chaim Gross's skylit ground-floor workspace. Squint your eyes and these marble and wood forms might be flamboyant actors, musicians, novelists, poets, and ballerinas attending a gallery opening – art-world denizens and darlings dressed in *de rigueur* New York black. Behind this raucous sculptural assemblage, the workbenches, overflowing cabinets, shelves, wooden stands, a wall of well-loved tools, and personal items remain just as they were during the sculptor's lifetime.

This is only the first floor of a wondrous four-story house a few blocks south of Washington Square. Chaim Gross and his wife Renee lived on the three upper floors and filled their private residence with an extraordinary art collection acquired during their 59-year marriage. On every wall, shelf, and tabletop of the third floor – and lining every stairwell - you see outstanding drawings, photographs (Marilyn Monroe, Helen Keller, Sigmund Freud), sculptures, and paintings by Gross's friends and contemporaries (DeKooning, Grosz, Picasso, Leger, Soyer). American and European masterworks commingle with African and Oceanic carvings, pre-Columbian and Asian treasures, and showcases full of rare stone, clay, wood, and metal figurines. A second-floor public gallery displays temporary installations drawn from the Gross's collection. And the third floor's splendid front room – with art everywhere – is a modern-day *salon* where special readings, lectures, and talks take place.

In some respects, this personal collection outshines the art displayed in many museums. But Renee and Chaim Gross valued their privacy, so unless you know the address or happen to spot the foundation's discreet sign inside the front gate, you could easily miss this not-to-be-missed experience of creative energy and inspiration.

Address 526 LaGuardia Place (between Bleecker and West 3rd Street), New York 10012, Phone +1 212.529.4906, www.rcgrossfoundation.org | Transit Subway: Bleecker St (6); W 4 St (A, B, C, D, E, F, M); Prince St (N, R), Bus: M1, M2, M5, M8, M21, M103 | Hours Thu – Fri 1 – 5pm, or by appointment | Tip *The Family*, a bronze statue at Bleecker & West 11th Street, was Chaim Gross's gift to the city in honor of Mayor Edward Koch.

17___Championship Play
On the world's largest chessboard

Wander through New York's parks and outdoor plazas and you're likely to come upon clusters of passionate chess devotees hunched over their boards contemplating strategy for the decisive next move. Walk down the 48th Street side of the towering building at 767 Third Avenue and look up to see a massive, three-story-high chessboard mounted on a wall that's visible to, and is a beloved open-air extension of, the building's lobby. The casual passer-by might smile, thinking it a quirky bit of urban decor, but this is the real deal. Every Wednesday at noon, since its installation in 1982, a worker perched on a cherry-picker shifts a 2.5-foot-round chess piece to recreate a move from a historic match. A flag at the left of the board identifies which side has the next move and a brass plaque invites the viewer to guess which side will win. A sign prominently displayed inside the lobby provides the curious visitor with a detailed description of the legendary game in progress and offers a prize to the first person to submit the correct solution.

Visionary design guru Melvyn Kaufman collaborated with prominent architects and designers of the day to spice up several midtown and downtown buildings owned by his father's development firm. He detested the sterile marble-walled public spaces that were the style at the time and expressed his unique personal philosophy with what the *New York Times* called "a combination of sleek modernism and Disneyesque ornamentation." He insisted the lobbies and public spaces of his buildings engage the wonder, excitement, and whimsy of both tenants and passers-by. His peers often considered him eccentric, yet this master of combining modern glass-and-steel skyscrapers with interactive play was decades ahead of his time.

Sit on a wooden bench in the plaza below this massive chessboard, contemplate your next move, and match wits with the best.

Address 767 Third Avenue (on East 48th Street), New York 10022 | Transit Subway: 51 St (6); Lexington Av-53 St (N, Q, R), Bus: M15, M42, M50, M101, M102, M103 | Hours Daily 24 hours | Tip More Kaufman building surprises at 747 Third Avenue, home to a statue of a nude woman briefly visible through revolving doors at its entrance; 777 Third Avenue; 77 Water Street; and 127 John Street.

18__ The Chelsea Hotel

If the walls could speak, the tales they'd tell

More than a building, the Chelsea is a living chrysalis, an eccentric cocoon nurturing generations of geniuses and oddballs. Known to painters, writers, filmmakers, and musicians for over a century, it was the most free-style (and cheapest) place to stay in NYC, where kindred spirits mingled and creativity flourished.

The guest register is a *Who's Who* of artistic brilliance. Here Jack Kerouac wrote *On the Road*; Bob Dylan penned *Sad-Eyed Lady of the Lowlands*; Madonna photographed her book *Sex*; Leonard Cohen composed *Chelsea Hotel #2* (about Janis Joplin); Arthur C. Clarke wrote *2001: A Space Odyssey*; and Arthur Miller recovered from his split with Marilyn. Mark Twain, Sarah Bernhardt, Jimi Hendrix, Andy Warhol, Frida Kahlo, Allen Ginsberg, Iggy Pop, Brendan Behan, Simone de Beauvoir, Tennessee Williams, Stanley Kubrick, Dee Dee Ramone, Jackson Pollock – they all slept here.

Opened in 1884 as not only NYC's tallest structure and largest residential building, but a social experiment. Architect Philip Hubert believed communal living across economic classes could cure societal woes. So he designed diverse living quarters: small working-class flats, grand residences for the rich, painters' studios, plus common areas (parlors, roof garden, restaurant) where all could mix. When that utopian model failed financially, it reopened as a hotel in 1905, and became an ideal haven for bohemian life.

Stanley Bard, owner-manager from the late 1960s to 2007, coddled this scandalous clubhouse, often accepting paintings from struggling artists (later world-famous) in lieu of rent. He covered the walls with museum-worthy art. Bard would tell guests who came for a week that they'd never leave. Decrying plans to transform it into a boutique hotel, many longtime residents now refuse to move.

Here Dylan Thomas fell into a fatal coma and Sid Vicious' girlfriend was murdered. Ghosts abound... and why would they leave?

Address 222 West 23rd Street (between Seventh and Eighth Avenue), New York 10011, www.chelseahotels.com | **Transit** Subway: 23 St (1, C, E, F, M, N, R), Bus: M 5, M 7, M 11, M 20, M 23 | **Tip** Next door at Doughnut Plant NYC, try house-made pastry treats like *creme brulee*, peanut butter & blackberry jam, and chocolate blackout.

19__Chico Murals

Transformative street art

Walk through the Lower East Side around Avenues A, B, C, and D and you'll notice brightly painted murals that crop up in unexpected places – crumbling cement walls, store facades, metal security gates, and alleys. Almost every image in this inspiring open-air art gallery was created by the extremely prolific street artist Antonio Garcia, whose mom nicknamed him Chico when he was a kid. Chico's signature 'tag' appears on hundreds of colorful paintings that raise social consciousness and offer messages of hope to residents of run-down streets in Loisaida (*Spanglish* for Lower East Side), Spanish Harlem, and the Bronx. He's the city's best-known contemporary muralist and a beloved neighborhood celebrity.

Chico grew up in public housing on Avenue D and began his artist's career in the late 1970s, sneaking into locked train yards late at night to spray-paint graffiti on subway cars. One of the city's first spray-can artists, he'd readily spend his entire paycheck (from his job at NYC's Housing Authority) to buy paint. His talent and skill has flourished for more than three decades with street art that encompasses a wildly expressive visual vocabulary. Some Chico murals pay tribute to recognizable inspirational figures – JFK, Mother Teresa, the Pope, pop stars, and sports heroes. Others portray street people and local history, personal tragedies and community celebrations. Bereaved families have commissioned him to memorialize loved ones whose lives were lost through violence, while local grocers and bar owners hire him to depict landscapes, animals, or urban scenes on their storefronts.

His graffiti and street art was featured in the movie *Rent* and has appeared on the streets and in galleries of Tokyo, London, Amsterdam, and Rome. And despite rumors of spray-paint fumes making him crazy, Chico's creativity is very much intact and he continues to produce provocative, uplifting art.

Address Most Chico murals are located on and around Avenues A, B, C, and D, and side streets from 1st to 14th Street. | **Transit** Subway: 1 Av (L); 2 Av (F), Bus: M 8, M 9, M 14A, M 14D, M 21 | **Tip** Order corned beef on rye at Katz's Delicatessen, where the hilarious faked-orgasm scene in *When Harry Met Sally* was filmed.

20__ The Chinese Immigrant Experience

MOCA, an American story

One door is in Chinatown and the other is in SoHo. Symbolically, artist Maya Lin's design for MOCA, the Museum of Chinese in America, straddles old and new to express Chinese-American history, culture, dreams, and identity.

At its heart is a skylit brick atrium – it might be a courtyard in a traditional Chinese home or alley walls between tenements. Galleries are arranged around this core space, with video portraits of illustrious Chinese-Americans projected on suspended panels. The translucent, almost ghostly faces seem to magically encounter each other, reaching across the courtyard – and across decades.

In the lobby, the Journey Wall's bronze tiles are engraved in both Chinese and English with family names, place of origin in China, and where they settled in the US. In the main gallery called *With A Single Step*, floor-to-ceiling interactive exhibits bring to life 160 years of the Chinese-American experience. Share the history: open a desk drawer revealing a child's bilingual schoolbook; read ads and posters imposing cruel stereotypes; sit in a stiff-backed interrogation chair. See a once-familiar neon sign for Chop Suey (strictly an American invention). View newsreels like *China Fights Back!* (during its war with Japan). Photos, letters, documents, clippings, films, and recordings honor those who helped make America: railroad builders to laundry and restaurant workers to scholars. And admire those who 'made it': film star Anna May Wong, farmer Ah Bing (Bing cherries!), cellist Yo Yo Ma, Olympic skater Michelle Kwan, architect I.M. Pei.

Another gallery recreates a combined general store/post office/ travel agency – a vital lifeline for immigrant families to connect with relatives in China and Chinatowns across the US. Through MOCA's innovative school programs and events like films, festivals, readings, and tours, the American story continues.

Address 215 Centre Street (between Howard and Grand Street), New York 10013, Phone +1 212.619.4785, www.mocanyc.org, info@mocanyc.org | **Transit** Subway: Canal St (6, N, R, Q, J, Z), Bus: M 5, M 9, M 15, M 22, M 103 | **Hours** Tue, Wed and Fri – Sun 11am – 6pm, Thu 11am – 9pm, closed Mon | **Tip** At 239 Centre (4th floor) browse thru Posteritati, an archive of over 9,000 international movie posters, including an original *King Kong*, with prices from $20 to $75,000.

21 Chrysler Building Lobby

A triangular gem

The Chrysler Building is the shining star of Manhattan's skyline. Illuminated after dark, its radiant stainless steel spire glitters like a jeweled tiara. Exterior details – many inspired by the design elements of Chrysler automobiles of the 1920s – resemble car-radiator caps, wheel hubs, and hood ornaments, as well as winged urns, eagles, sunbursts, and gargoyles. Yet the crowning glory of this iconic tower is actually at street level, inside the surprisingly triangular, and most elaborate lobby in the entire city. This Art Deco palace, on the city's main thoroughfare of 42nd Street, is the embodiment of the American *zeitgeist* of that period – with rapid industrialization, emerging new technologies, and faith in social progress.

Edward Turnbull's massive mural on the lobby's ceiling (one of the world's largest paintings) is titled *Energy, Result, Workmanship, and Transportation.* Crane your neck, walk slowly beneath to examine its planes, trains, ocean liners, machines, and teams of workers (with faces of actual tradesmen who built the skyscraper).

The lobby's mesmerizing interior orchestrates a symphony of swirling colors, geometric shapes, smooth, shiny surfaces, and exotic materials – red African marble walls, yellow Siena marble floor, blue marble and amber onyx trim. Sleek chrome accents and machine-age imagery nearly overwhelm the senses. Peek into one of the four elevator banks. The doors of each of its thirty-two elevators are unforgettable masterpieces of inlaid wood marquetry, employing rare varieties of wood to give a spectacular Deco spin to Egyptian lotus-flower motifs.

When it opened in 1930, the Chrysler Building was the tallest structure in the world for a few months (soon eclipsed by the Empire State). But its lofty ambitions, social message, heroism, and roll-up-your-sleeves optimism are grounded to this day in one of New York's precious treasures – its lobby.

Address 405 Lexington Avenue (at 42nd Street), New York 10174 | **Transit** Subway: Grand Central-42 St (4, 5, 6, 7, S), Bus: M 1, M 2, M 3, M 4, M 42, M 101, M 102, M 103 | **Hours** Mon – Fri 8am – 6pm | **Tip** Get a stunning view of the Chrysler Building and its namesake cocktail at Upstairs, a rooftop lounge at the Kimberly Hotel (145 East 50th Street).

22__City Reliquary

Persistence of memorabilia

This storefront resembling a neighborhood bodega is actually a mini-museum, an enchanted portal to an adventurous expedition through ordinary – and extraordinary – NYC history. An abundance of delightful and peculiar city artifacts, collectibles, improbable treasures, and impossible-to-categorize stuff is crammed onto walls and shelves, floor to ceiling, in display cases, atop tables and every available surface.

Nostalgia rules the day: a Chinatown newsstand rescued from the trash heap; equipment from an old-time barbershop; a dusty, decomposing display cake from the window of a defunct Brooklyn bakery. Here to tell stories more personal and profound than those in the city's grander cultural institutions are old seltzer bottles, World's Fair mementos (from both '39 and '64 Fairs), souvenir Statues of Liberty, bits of buildings and bedrock, salvaged signage, and ephemera of every description.

It began in 2002 when firefighter Dave Herman displayed in his ground-floor Brooklyn apartment window a whimsical assortment of NYC items and a homemade directory of local landmarks. Word spread, and over the next four years folks from the neighborhood, all five boroughs, and ex-pat New Yorkers donated personal keepsakes to Dave's eccentric accumulation. In 2006, the expanded collection was moved to its own location, becoming The City Reliquary, a community museum and civic organization, complete with a board of directors and volunteer staff.

Visitors enter the idiosyncratic museum through a vintage subway turnstile. In an adjoining room, temporary exhibitions focus on exceptional aspects of life, work, and art of the city – and anyone can apply to exhibit. The backyard hosts special events, screenings, concerts, and parties. Amusing local souvenirs in the gift shop include a rubber replica of the NYC Croton bug (a giant cockroach) and the urban-legend sewer alligator. Only in New York!

Address 370 Metropolitan Avenue (at Havemeyer Street), Brooklyn, New York 11211, **Phone** +1 718.782.4842, www.cityreliquary.org | **Transit** Subway: Metropolitan Av (G), Lorimer St (L), Marcy Av (J, M), Bus: B 24, B 62, Q 59 | **Hours** Thu – Sun noon – 6pm | **Tip** Reminisce down the street at Radegast Hall & Biergarten, an Austro-Hungarian *bier haus* and dining hall in the shell of two historic warehouses.

SELTZER BOTTLES ∞ BROOKLYN

23 The City's Heart of Gold
Gold vault at the NY Federal Reserve

The Federal Reserve Bank building resembles a fortress for good reason – its basement houses a vault that stores and guards 7,000 tons of gold currently valued at $360 billion! The world's largest known depository of gold sits undisturbed eighty feet underground, surrounded by Manhattan bedrock.

Security? Over a hundred cage-like numbered compartments are protected by multiple locks and an auditor's seal within the 9-foot-tall, 90-ton steel vault; all this is inside a 140-ton steel-and-concrete, air- and water-tight sealed frame. Once the vault-entrance locking bolts are activated, they cannot be unlocked until the next business day. An elaborate, ever-vigilant, 24-hour monitoring system includes security cameras, motion sensors, and the Fed's own armed police force.

Ninety-eight percent of the entombed gold is foreign-owned. Proprietorship is kept strictly confidential. The largest holder has 107,000 bars, the smallest just a single one. Complete inventory is taken weekly. Only governments, central banks, and official international organizations (not individuals) are permitted to keep gold here. Storage is free. Most current holdings were deposited during and after World War II, when NYC was deemed the most secure place to store the world's gold reserves. So it was a real thriller when it got fictionally ravaged in the 1995 hit movie *Die Hard with a Vengeance*.

Visit the vault when you take NY Federal Reserve Bank's free guided tour. Reserve online, print out your personalized admission ticket, and bring photo ID. You'll learn about the history of the Federal Reserve and its stated mission to oversee our financial system, support a healthy economy, regulate banks, distribute currency, process checks and electronic payments. Then, descending five floors below street level, you'll find yourself literally face-to-face with New York's goldmine.

Address 44 Maiden Lane (between Nassau and William Street), New York 10045,
www.ny.frb.org/aboutthefed/visiting.html | Transit Subway: Wall St (2, 3); Fulton St (4, 5,
A, C, J); Cortlandt St (R), Bus: M 5, M 9, M 15, M 22, M 103 | Hours Tours Mon – Fri 1pm
and 2pm (except bank holidays) | Tip Look for the working century-old clock embedded
in the sidewalk at the intersection of Maiden Lane & Broadway.

24＿Coney Island Circus Sideshow

Weirdness and wonder

Grab yourself a Nathan's hot dog and stroll over to Sideshows by the Seashore to watch live sword swallowers, fire breathers, snake charmers, contortionists, escape artists, and talented 'born different' performers. This New York landmark in the heart of Brooklyn's Coney Island is a traditional ten-acts-in-one spectacle that pays homage to its roots in vaudeville, burlesque, Houdini, and P. T. Barnum.

You can't miss the funky white-and-blue building decorated with vibrant posters and cartoon signage painted by Coney Island Museum artists. Inside you'll see whimsical banners, neon signs, event posters, and an assortment of unusual items on the walls and ceiling. As you wait for the performance to start, browse memorabilia and curiosities inside the museum, buy a bizarre souvenir or t-shirt in the shop, and have a drink under the hammerhead shark suspended over the bar.

The show begins as a dapper gent wearing a straw hat opens the door and ushers you into a small, somewhat seedy theater with wooden bleacher seats facing a dimly lit stage. A general grittiness makes it feel raunchy and authentic. An emcee steps onstage, surveying the audience. Cracking jokes and making ironic comments, he presents a weird yet charismatic line-up of remarkable artists whose feats can amaze you or make you cringe and cover your eyes in horror.

This is theater with a twist. Spikes get hammered through noses. Knives, swords, flames, and super-long balloons are swallowed whole. A lady trapped in a box is skewered with blades. An audience-member volunteer is electrified. A diminutive one-man-band rock musician performs from a wheelchair, and invites personal questions from the audience.

Perpetuating the rich history of the American sideshow, one of our earliest forms of theater, these performances are not just nostalgic – they're modern, thrilling, and enormously entertaining.

Address 1208 Surf Avenue (between West 12th Street and Stillwell Avenue), Brooklyn, New York 11224, Phone +1 718.372.5159, www.coneyisland.com, info@coneyisland.com | **Transit** Subway: Coney Island-Stillwell Av (D, F, N, Q), Bus: B 36, B 64, B 68, B 74, B 82 | **Hours** Daily 1–8pm, from mid-June to Labor Day. Website posts spring and Sep. schedules; call to confirm hours. | **Tip** In daytime, take a walk on the boardwalk to the New York Aquarium. On Friday nights all summer, thrill to fireworks on the beach.

25 — Croquet in the Park

A wicket way to spend the day

Peek through the fence at a manicured lawn where players dressed in white from head to toe whack colorful balls with wooden sticks. Curious crowds gather to watch, and folks new to the game try to puzzle out its rules. Chatting with players on the sidelines you'll get to know croquet, a sociable pastime – and often seriously competitive sport – that's been played on these courts since 1972.

The sticks are called mallets, hoops on the ground are wickets, and the idea is to knock the balls through the wickets. What looks simple actually requires great skill. In *Alice in Wonderland* the Queen of Hearts' mallet was a live flamingo and a hedgehog was the ball. Today's players are more civilized, their equipment less fantastical, but competition can still be fierce.

The game's origins date back to eleventh-century France's *jeu de mail*, borrowed three centuries later by the British, and developed by the Irish into croquet as it's played today. Modifications made by Scots created the game of golf. King Louis XIV's displeasure at his inability to play outdoors in winter gave rise to an indoor variation – known to us as billiards.

Competitive croquet in the US began with the establishment of the New York Croquet Club in 1967. Its members are men and women of all ages and backgrounds, from stockbrokers to students. It's one of the few sports in which both sexes play with a similar handicap. Many players on the court are champions who compete in national and international tournaments. Members get a Parks Department permit to play on the court and keys to its front gate and adjacent clubhouse. If you're interested in learning the game or brushing up on rusty skills, take a free lesson from an expert any fair-weather Monday evening, May through October. White attire isn't required for a lesson but flat-soled shoes are a must.

Discover croquet's home in Central Park and have fun swinging a mean mallet.

Address Enter the park at West 69th Street, Central Park West, New York 10023, Phone +1 917.310.8724, www.newyorkcroquetclub.com, nycroquetclub@yahoo.com | **Transit** Subway: 66 St-Lincoln Center (1); 72 St (1, 2, 3); 59 St-Columbus Circle (A, B, C, D), Bus: M 5, M 7, M 10, M 20, M 66, M 72, M 104 | **Hours** May – Oct. 8am – dusk; free instruction Mondays 6pm – dusk | **Tip** Le Pain Quotidien, steps from the croquet court, serves *tartines*, French pastry, and iced hibiscus tea for your picnic in the Sheep Meadow.

26__Cupcake ATM
Swipe here for sweetness

It's the middle of the night: 2am, your pregnant wife gets that crazy craving. 3am, party's over, you danced and drank too much, and you're suddenly possessed by a gnawing ache. 5am, your roomie awakens from that recurring Willy Wonka dream, his sweet tooth sounds an urgent alarm. You recognize the desperate feeling. But at that ungodly hour how do you get your sugar rush? Problem solved: jump in a cab and head to the ATM across from Bloomingdale's. Not for cash, silly . . . for a cupcake!

Peruse a parade of mouthwatering flavors on a touch-screen just like your bank's ATM. The procedure is simple, but selecting only one cupcake from the great variety could slow you down. Can't choose between cinnamon sugar, lemon coconut, and banana dark chocolate? Get them all! They even have made-for-dogs mini-cupcakes to bring home a treat for your favorite pooch. The machine can dispense up to four selections at a time. Make your choice, swipe your credit card (sorry, cash not accepted) and *voila!* – a door slides open and your tasty treasure is delivered in a neat pink-and-brown box. Tear it open for sweet satisfaction and a yummy buzz.

Sprinkles, a Beverly Hills-based bakery focused on fabulous gourmet cupcakes, was a major incubator for the current US cupcake craze. The idea for a 24-hour ATM was hatched when founder Candace Nelson was pregnant and, yes, craved cupcakes late at night. So the ATM is open around the clock, 365 days a year, offering twenty rotating varieties of fresh-baked, devilishly delicious cupcakes (the machine holds about eight hundred of them!) made to delight night owls with midnight munchies, gourmet go-getters, busy bees, scurrying shoppers, and anyone who just plain adores machines that dispense 'stuff.'

During the day, at your leisure, take an up-close look at the delectable daily variety baked right next door at Sprinkles' walk-in shop.

Address 780 Lexington Avenue (between East 60th and 61st Street), New York 10065, www.sprinkles.com/cupcake-atm, atm@sprinkles.com | **Transit** Subway: Lexington Av-59 St (4,5,6,N,Q,R), Bus: M 1, M 2, M 3, M 4, M 15, M 31, M 57, M 68, M 101, M 102, M 103 | **Hours** Always open, 24/7 | **Tip** Further indulge your sweet tooth at nearby Dylan's Candy Bar, founded by the daughter of fashion designer Ralph Lauren.

27__ The Dakota

Storied stories

Wherever you're from, it's likely you've heard of The Dakota, once home to John Lennon and Yoko Ono where, on a tragic day in 1980, Lennon was gunned down. Fans visit the building's gate to take photos, leave mementos and place flowers, and pay tribute at the *Imagine* memorial across the street in Central Park. You may also know the thriller *Rosemary's Baby*, in which The Dakota's creepier architectural details heighten suspense.

Built in the 1880s, The Dakota was situated miles from the city's residential areas where many of its wealthy owned townhouses. It was the brainchild of developer Edward Clark, president of Singer Sewing Machines, who gambled on a then-extraordinary notion that the affluent would live in a multiple-dwelling structure. It offered appealing economic advantages: reduced domestic staff, greater security, shared amenities like central heating and concierge service, and a private inner garden with croquet and tennis courts. Its formidable exterior blended German Gothic, French Renaissance, and English Victorian styles – with gables, dormers, balconies, turrets, and ornate stone and ironwork trim. Each of the sixty-five grand high-ceilinged apartments was unique, with spectacular vistas and rich adornments. Clark's own residence had floors inlaid with silver. As the city's first luxury apartment building, it stoked the aesthetic sensibilities of high society. By opening day all residences had been rented – the building was a huge social success.

The Dakota, declared a National Historic Landmark in 1976, remains a sanctuary for cultural icons and the privileged. High-profile residents have included Andrew Carnegie, Boris Karloff, Carson McCullers, Judy Garland, Lauren Bacall, Rudolf Nureyev, John Madden, and Leonard Bernstein. Its idiosyncratic apartments are still highly prized, with dramatic Central Park views and a strong whiff of history and mystery.

Address 1 West 72nd Street (between Central Park West and Columbus Avenue), New York 10023 | **Transit** Subway: 72 St (A, B, C, 1, 2, 3); 66 St-Lincoln Center (1, 2), Bus: M 10, M 11, M 72 | **Tip** Legend has it The Dakota's name came from its remote location (as far as the Dakota territories), but actually Clark had an affinity for the new territories out west. Find a Dakota Indian atop the 72nd Street facade and other Upper West Side buildings with western or Native American names carved on their facades.

28_ The Dinner Party
A seat at the table

In a dark and starry space that seems to extend beyond all boundaries sits a monumental, fully-set banquet table forming an open equilateral triangle. It's firmly grounded yet infinitely reflected. At first it's dazzling, almost too immense. As your eyes adjust to the darkness and scale of the gallery, the details reveal why this iconic work, *The Dinner Party*, is a milestone in feminist art.

The ceremonial table lays out place settings for thirty-nine mythical and historical women, thirteen on each of its 48-foot-long sides. Each setting has a cloth table runner embroidered with the guest-of-honor's name and patterns or imagery that symbolize her life; a golden chalice and utensils; and most prominent, a sculpted ceramic dinner plate (fashioned in vulvar and butterfly forms) representing her essence. At the room's center is the glistening, tiled *Heritage Floor* – gold-inscribed names of 999 women who were left out of history books but whose lives inspired those at the table.

Artist Judy Chicago's original plan was to paint images of great ladies on china plates. It evolved into an elaborate five-year project commemorating significant women in Western civilization through embroidery, weaving, and china-decoration – traditional 'women's work' emblematic of oppression and domestication. Chicago described her mission to reclaim these lost histories as "a reinterpretation of the Last Supper from the point of view of women who, throughout history, prepared the meals and set the table." Hundreds of volunteer artisans – ceramicists, weavers, calligraphers, researchers – collaborated to bring the artist's vision to life. First exhibited in 1979, it traveled the world. It now has a permanent home at the core of the Center for Feminist Art at the Brooklyn Museum.

From Primordial Goddess to Georgia O'Keeffe, women who command a place at the table nobly challenge you to partake.

Address Brooklyn Museum: Elizabeth A. Sackler Center for Feminist Art, 200 Eastern Parkway (at Washington Avenue), Brooklyn, New York 11238, Phone +1 718.638.5000, www.brooklynmuseum.org | **Transit** Subway: Eastern Pkwy-Brooklyn Museum (2, 3); Franklin Av (4, 5), Bus: B 41, B 45, B 48, B 69 | **Hours** Wed and Fri – Sun 11am – 6pm (first Sat every month 11am – 11pm), Thu 11am – 10pm, closed Mon and Tue | **Tip** Powerful female images from antiquity are in the museum's Egyptian Collection. The terracotta *Bird Lady* figurine is world famous.

29___The Drag Show at Lips
Boys will be girls

Judging by its chic exterior masquerading as an exclusive men's club – black canopy, elegant wood paneling, and beveled-glass doors framed by carriage lanterns – you'd expect Lips to be a sophisticated *boîte* where upper-crust patrons feast on *foie gras* and sip fine wine. Ah, but it's a clever trick. This self-proclaimed "Disneyland of Drag" is really a glitzy palace of glamour and gaiety. Inside its classy entrance, instead of a dining room fit for a king you'll encounter a raucous Las-Vegas-meets-Barbie-Dream-House full of gorgeous queens!

Curvaceous drag queen divas in extravagant, over-the-top, sequined and bejeweled costumes, with glam-fabulous makeup and spectacular coiffures impersonate legendary musical and theatrical icons, performing comedy, songs, and dance routines live on stage. They serve you food and drink *('The more you drink, the better we look!')*, engage in saucy banter, sit on your lap, and do their bosomy best to tickle your … um, fancy.

It's always hilarious fun. Nightly shows like Drag Karaoke, Bitchy Bingo, Queens of Drag, Dinner with the Divas, and Superstar Sundays are crowd-pleasers, delighting a widely diverse audience of men and women – native New Yorkers, commuters from the boroughs and surrounding suburbs, and fun-loving tourists. Sunday's show-stopping Broadway Brunch, hosted by the fab-dazzling Ginger Snapt, is so popular it's a good idea to book your table two weeks in advance! Come with a sweetheart, friends, or adventurous co-workers. Large groups are welcome, just call ahead to reserve. Lips is a sensational place for birthdays, bachelorette parties, or anything worthy of a memorable celebration.

Named-for-divas cocktails are featured on the drinks menu – like brain-freezing Yvonne Lamé Frozen Cosmo. The food is tasty, served in super-sized dinner and brunch portions. And while dinner's delightful, the divas are even more delicious. *Oh boy!*

Address 227 East 56th Street (between Second and Third Avenue), New York 10022, Phone +1 212.675.7710, www.lipsnyc.com | **Transit** Subway: Lexington Av-53 St (E, M); 51 St (6); Lexington Av-59 St (4, 5, 6, N, R); Lexington Av-63 St (F), Bus: M 1, M 2, M 3, M 4, M 15, M 31, M 57, M 101, M 102, M 103 | **Hours** Call or see website for specific daily show times. | **Tip** A world of glitter and glamour is at Tiffany's Fifth Avenue flagship store (at 57th Street), but they don't serve breakfast.

30_ The Dream House
Frequencies in sound and light

Press the third-floor buzzer, climb a steep stairway. Remove your shoes. Incense lures you to a space bathed in warm magenta light. The room is bare, a few cushions scattered on a soft carpeted floor. Droning vibrations resonate within your body. The space is so infused with sound and light, you feel compelled to sit or lie down so your entire being, all your senses, can soak it in. A small shrine to the Hindu singer Pandit Pran Nath invites meditation at the front; windows masked in dark translucence glow at the back. Curlicues suspended from the ceiling slowly turn, casting mystifying shadows on the walls. Drawn into the sensations, you become immersed in a transcendent experience.

This environment at the MELA Foundation is a collaboration between avant-garde composer La Monte Young and his wife, visual artist Marian Zazeela. MELA, an acronym for Music, Eternal Light and Art, is also the Sanskrit word for *harmonizing*. Young's "sound waveforms" derive from his lifelong study of harmonics, frequencies, and traditional Indian vocal technique. They combine seamlessly with Zazeela's symmetrical compositions of vibrating light and hue. Detect subtle shifting colors, follow moving shapes, marvel at improbable three-dimensional shadows. A narrow hallway illuminated by Zazeela's neon art leads to a smaller, even more intimate sound-filled, magenta-soaked space. Meditate, cogitate, recline, relax. Breathe.

Dream House was conceived in 1969, intended as a short-term art exhibit in Munich. It has often been reimagined in galleries across the world prior to its 1993 permanent installation in Tribeca, where the couple pioneered the loft movement in that then-grimy, now-thriving downtown area.

The Dream House website posts upcoming concerts, classes, and talks by Young & Zazeela, contemporary musicians, artists, philosophers, and spiritual teachers. Get in touch with your inner self.

Address 275 Church Street (between Franklin and White Street), New York 10013, Phone +1 212.925.8270, www.melafoundation.org, mail@melafoundation.org | **Transit** Subway: Franklin St (1); Canal St (A, C, E, J, N, Q, R, Z, 6), Bus: M 5, M 20, M 22 | **Hours** Wed – Sat 2pm – midnight | **Tip** Take a photo of FDNY Hook & Ladder 8 (14 North Moore Street), the firehouse that served as headquarters in *Ghostbusters*.

31 Driving Along the Hudson

The Golf Club at Chelsea Piers

Cross the busy West Side Highway alongside the Hudson River and navigate past a constant flow of runners, skaters, and bicyclists to reach Chelsea Piers, a world-class sports complex unlike any in the city. From studio yoga to large-scale sports – ice hockey, soccer, sailing – there's even golf.

The Golf Club's Pier 59 entryway is through an indoor garage, where you behold a sight you'd never expect on the city docks – the gabled roof and bay windows of a golf course clubhouse looking just like a typical suburban country club. This venue is an unexpected haven for golf-obsessed New Yorkers and visitors craving a fix – whether duffers or pros. Players at all levels, even juniors, can learn, practice, and perfect their game here.

The Club's 2,000-square-foot area is year-round, oblivious to the weather. Its outdoor driving range has 52 sheltered, heated stalls on four levels, facing a 200-yard-long net-enclosed 'fairway' perched over the river. Each stall has an automatic tee-up system delivering one ball at a time. Rent clubs or bring your own, then purchase either a number of balls or a block of time (a play-card activates the ball machine). Swing away, compare strokes with golfers in neighboring stalls, or take a lesson with the Club's PGA and LPGA teaching pros. You can play all winter – rates are lower, it's less crowded, and stalls are warm; when snow covers the artificial turf, a ground crew is quick to clear it away.

The Club is equipped with a 1,200-square-foot putting green, a chipping area, and sand trap. There are two full-swing simulators, where you can play a virtual round on one of fifty-five world-famous championship courses, like Pebble Beach or St. Andrews.

Come with friends or bring a special date at sunset for one of the most romantic views in town – and have a swinging evening.

Address Pier 59 (West 18th Street and Eleventh Avenue), New York 10011, Phone +1 212.336.6400, www.chelseapiers.com/gc, golfclub@chelseapiers.com | **Transit** Subway: 23 St (1, C, E), Bus: M 11, M 12, M 14D, M 23 | **Hours** Mar.–Oct. daily 6:30am–midnight; Nov.–Feb. daily 6:30am–11pm | **Tip** Put on a pair of ice skates and practice your figure-8's at Chelsea Piers' Sky Rink, with its panoramic views of the river.

32 Duke Ellington Stands Tall

Tribute to a jazz pioneer

At the intersection of Fifth Avenue and 110th Street, straddling a mostly white Upper East Side and a mostly black Harlem, is a monument to a monumental figure in American music. His artistic genius bridged the intersections of color and culture to overcome borders – real and perceived – across streets in New York and around the world.

Edward Kennedy 'Duke' Ellington – composer, pianist, bandleader, and consummate performer – was a towering presence. This 25-foot-high cast bronze statue, perched at the northernmost tip of Central Park, depicts a larger-than-life icon. Three slender pillars, each surrounded by three nude female figures (representing the nine Muses) extend skyward to support a gilded disc upon which the 8-foot-tall, elegantly-attired Ellington poses in his familiar stance beside a grand piano.

The composer of enduring classics like *Satin Doll, Take the A Train,* and *Caravan* was born in Washington, D.C., but he called New York home. Credited with elevating jazz to an art form, he resisted being called a jazz musician. He created more than a thousand musical compositions, alone and in collaboration with others, that defied and transcended genre labels. He considered himself an American musician "beyond category."

Establishing a tribute to Ellington was the idea of a lifelong admirer, celebrated cabaret singer and pianist Bobby Short. In 1979 he set up the Duke Ellington Memorial Fund, money was quickly raised, and Los Angeles artist Robert Graham was selected. But Short then spent eighteen frustrating years wrangling with city agencies to get the statue installed in its present location. When it was dedicated in 1997, among the honored guests and luminaries were Ellington's family and three NYC mayors.

If you're in town on the Sunday nearest April 29th, enjoy the annual birthday tribute to The Maestro at his statue.

Address Duke Ellington Circle (Fifth Avenue at 110th Street) | Transit Subway: 110 St (2, 3, 6), Bus: M 1, M 2, M 3, M 4, M 101, M 102, M 103 M 106 | Tip Borrow a fishing pole and get free bait at Central Park's Discovery Center (north shore of Harlem Meer, near 110th Street). It's home to the park's Catch-and-Release Fishing Program.

33___The Dyckman Farmhouse
Dutch treat

At the top of the island of Manhattan, in a place called Inwood, sits a storybook farmhouse atop a little hill on busy, noisy Broadway. It's such an anomaly, it might have been plunked down from the clouds. People passing by, running to catch a bus or taking kids to school, appear unaware of it. Indeed, the Dyckman Farmhouse may be visible only to visitors.

To enter its world, ascend a flowery path, climb a few steps to the front porch, and knock at the door. A welcoming staff member will greet you with a quick orientation to the only Dutch farmhouse still standing in Manhattan. You're invited to explore.

The rooms are cozy and charming, with original wide-plank chestnut floors. The formal parlor, dining room, two bedrooms, and winter kitchen each display authentic period furniture, decor, and quaint personal items that were heirlooms of the family that built the farm in 1784 and lived there until 1871. The rear door opens onto a wide porch overlooking a half-acre backyard garden, all that's left of the original 250-acre farm. Lovingly tended landscaping, a flourishing flower garden, and a few small historic outdoor structures (a re-created smokehouse, an original military hut, and a well) evoke a genteel, bygone era. A framed genealogy in the dining room, *Dyckman Household c. 1820*, traces the family tree. Members of the Dyckman clan were among the earliest settlers in the remote northern region of what was then known as Mannahatta.

In 1915, no longer in family hands, the house was threatened with demolition. To ensure its preservation, two sisters – Dyckman descendants – bought, restored, and gifted it to the city. Today, owned by the NYC Parks Department and the Historic House Trust, the Dyckman Farmhouse Museum Alliance maintains the property, raising funds to support programs and events designed to engage dialogue between community members, history buffs, and local artists. Treat yourself!

Address 4881 Broadway (at West 204th Street), New York 10034, Phone 1+ 212.304.9422, www.dyckmanfarmhouse.org, info@dyckmanfarmhouse.org | Transit Subway: 207 St (1); Inwood-207 St (A), Bus: BXM 1, M 100, BX 7 | Hours Fri – Sun 11am – 5pm | Tip Walk a few blocks down Broadway to the northeast side of Ft. Tryon Park and take a steep hike up to the Cloisters. Hudson River views are worth the tough uphill trek.

34__Eddie's Shoeshine & Repair

Shoe love

They're like masters of the universe – impeccably-groomed, handsome men and women – who you imagine need only snap their fingers to get whatever they want. But these bigwigs from NBC, high-powered bankers, and the corporate elite – with pay packages as high as their Rockefeller Center tower suites – can be seen daily, patiently waiting in a line that snakes out the door of a small shoe repair shop on the building's lower Concourse level. So what lures them to leave the rarefied air at the top and descend below 30 Rock and its famed ice rink? Answer: one of five coveted seats at Eddie's, where polished professionals wax and buff shoes to a mirror shine that literally reflects success.

The good news is you don't have to be a VIP to join the line. For the price of a subway ride, anyone with shoes worth shining can take a seat on an elevated wood-and-leather throne, settle their feet on brass shoe rests, and get a shoeshine done right. When it's finally your turn, the manager shouts *Next!* and hands you a newspaper (traditionally the *NY Post*), then sends you to one of the much-prized armchairs.

Aromas of polish, wax, soap, and leather infuse the air. Read the news, check the latest stock market quotes on the flat screen TV, or delve into your smartphone apps while your shoes enjoy the undivided attention of an expert. After laces are removed and metal buckles shielded with masking tape, every nook and cranny of leather is cleaned, moisturized, and treated to successive rounds of applications, brushing, and buffing. And what a pleasurable sensation for the feet! Twenty minutes later, the transformation complete, your shoes look better than new and you feel like a million bucks.

Owner Hugo Ardaix is a stickler for perfection and his pro team of shoeshine artists, all attired in red shirts and beige aprons, take great pride in their work. You'll want to add a generous tip.

Address 30 Rockefeller Plaza (at 49th Street, between Fifth Avenue and Avenue of the Americas), Concourse Level, New York 10020, Phone +1 212.581.3463 | Transit Subway: 47-50 Sts-Rockefeller Ctr (B, D, F, M); 49 St (N, Q, R); 5th Av-53 St (E); 50 St (1), Bus: M1, M2, M3, M4, M5, M7, M50 | Hours Mon – Fri 7am – 6pm | Tip For a truly indulgent shave and a haircut, walk across the corridor and settle into the barber chair at eShave.

35__The Elevated Acre

Retreat from the street

Buttoned-up brokers, Wall Street wizards, and harried hedge-fund honchos escape the financial district's feverish pace, quietly unwinding at an idyllic park thirty feet above street level. The Elevated Acre is an antidote to stress – and possibly lower Manhattan's best-kept secret.

The approach is discreet. A small sign is easy to miss. Search for a pair of escalators sandwiched between 55 Water Street and the adjacent office tower. Ride up to the landing, then board another escalator to the top. Here, three stories up, you'll encounter a peaceful, fresh-air oasis that magically erases every trace of the rushing hordes and gray sidewalks below. Three spectacular, diverse landscapes combine to soothe the soul: a soft astroturf meadow; a woodsy glen with winding paths through trees, shrubs, and flower beds; and a riverfront promenade with sweeping panoramic views. Individual seating and tables are artfully arranged to offer tranquility and encourage private moments.

Kick off your shoes, stretch out on the all-season lawn and, with your briefcase as a pillow, count clouds in the sky. Or cuddle with your date – a cozy bench in a quiet niche is ideal for a lunchtime tryst. Picnic on the grass or fly a kite. Contemplate the universe, perched on wide steps that evoke an ancient amphitheater. Climb to the boardwalk platform atop the steps to enjoy vistas of sky and river, with a never-ending regatta of tugboats, ferries, and tall ships.

In the 1970s, developers got permits to build six floors higher on a new structure if public space was part of the design. A nondescript plaza was built at 55 Water Street to take advantage of the incentive. Fast forward thirty years, and this humdrum space has been transformed into a city treasure.

In tune with its Wall Street environs, the Elevated Acre focuses on mergers and acquisitions – merging with nature and acquiring inner peace.

Address 55 Water Street (between Old Slip and Broad Street), New York 10004 | Transit Subway: Whitehall St-South Ferry (R); South Ferry (1); Bowling Green (4, 5), Bus: M5, M15, M20 | Hours Daily 8am–9pm | Tip A shrine to the first American-born saint, Elizabeth Seton, is at the Church of Our Lady of the Holy Rosary at 7 State Street.

36 _ Elizabeth Street Garden

Offbeat urban oasis

Sandwiched between SoHo, Little Italy, and Greenwich Village, Nolita is a stroller's delight. Its streets abound with chic boutiques and cool bistros. On Elizabeth Street, between Spring and Prince, there's a whimsical-looking acre of green space that's often discovered by pure accident – just when you feel like taking a break in a tranquil setting. You've stumbled upon the Elizabeth Street Garden, an open, statue-filled oasis that extends through the block to Mott Street, inviting you to relax and refresh.

This vacant lot where a school once stood was leased from the city by the adjacent Elizabeth Street Gallery to store and display the shop's overflow. This fascinating antique shop, housed in an 1850s firehouse, is filled to the rafters with one-of-a-kind works of art and old relics. After taking over the outdoor space from the city and clearing piles of rubble and debris, an eclectic mix of statuary and architectural artifacts from the gallery's collection was installed and a beautiful community garden was created. Neighborhood volunteers planted and tended the park's grass, flowers, trees, and shrubs, and they continue to do so today as part of their ongoing commitment to preserving this space as a community park, despite continuing political pressure to repurpose it.

You can hear songbirds in the trees as you sit beside a rustic table or in the gazebo, reading poetry or checking your e-mail. In warm months the flowers and foliage are luxuriant, while winter snowfalls impart a special kind of magic. Wander along the garden paths and you'll undoubtedly smile at the quirky juxtaposition of styles, eras, and types of *objets d'art*. Ancient carved Greek and Roman urns perch amidst a menagerie of sphinxes, caryatids, lions, angels, wood nymphs, folk art curios, and salvaged architectural ironwork. It's both magnificent and amusing – and a perfect place to unwind from city life.

Address Elizabeth Street (between Prince and Spring Street), New York 10012, www.elizabethstreetgarden.org | Transit Subway: Bowery (J); Prince St (N, R); Spring St (6); Broadway-Lafayette St (B, D, F, M), Bus: M 5, M 15, M 21, M 103 | Hours Summer hours: daily noon – 6pm; Winter hours: Wed, Sat and Sun 11am – 3pm (weather permitting) | Tip Grab a table or counter seat at Cafe Habana on the corner of Prince Street for incomparable grilled corn and muddled-mint *mojitos*.

37_Enoteca Maria

Because nobody cooks like Nonna

Cuisine-crazed foodies post photos of their meals on social media and top chefs are now bona fide celebrities. Competition is fierce and food preparation increasingly complex. But after a while, jaded diners who hunt for the latest and greatest secretly just yearn for dinner at grandma's.

Each of Enoteca Maria's rotating cast of chefs is an authentic *nonna* (grandmother) who prepares traditional family recipes handed down through generations and puts her heart into every meal she cooks. At first, all were from Italy, recruited via ads in Italian newspapers. Today, while continuing to offer a nightly menu cooked by an Italian *nonna* – scrumptious regional dishes with aromas that would even make Mario Batali swoon – an alternative menu presents traditional specialties prepared by one of the *Nonnas of the World*. Home cooks from countries as diverse as Algeria, Ecuador, the Czech Republic, France, Kazakhstan, Poland, Colombia, and Belarus take turns throughout the week in a second kitchen.

Dinner at Enoteca Maria is a surefire way to dazzle a date. Board the (free!) Staten Island ferry at sunset – when pink, orange, and purple skies bathe lower Manhattan's skyline and the Statue of Liberty. Twenty-five minutes later you dock at what's been called New York's forgotten borough. A short stroll uphill through the historic district of St. George, and you're there. The vibe inside is cool and contemporary, a smart mix of rock, jazz, and world music sets the scene, marble tabletops shine, and wine glasses sparkle as hand-picked Italian wines are poured.

And the food! Every mouthwatering bite is bursting with love. "Ooh, try this!" you sigh, passing delectable forkfuls to each other across the table.

Proprietor and attentive host Jody Scaravella says it best: "If I have a choice between a three-star Michelin chef's restaurant and grandma's, I'm going to grandma's. I'm going right to the source."

Address 27 Hyatt Street, Staten Island, New York 10301, Phone +1 718.447.2777 (call for reservations), www.enotecamaria.com, info@enotecamaria.com | **Transit** to Staten Island Ferry: Subway: South Ferry (1); Bowling Green (4, 5); Whitehall St (R), Bus: M5, M15, M20; from Staten Island ferry terminal: Walk uphill on the street left of the clock tower. | **Hours** Wed – Sun 3pm until everyone goes home! | **Tip** Catch a headliner show at the restored St. George Theatre, a grand old movie and vaudeville house of the 1930s.

38 __ Essex Street Market

Taste tradition and nibble the new

One-stop shopping is big here, with a huge array of edible treats you'd otherwise have to hunt down all over town, and diverse merchants you wouldn't think could coexist under one roof. Mom-and-pop grocers, many there for decades, sell oxtails, oranges, cuchifritos, and couscous, next to booths run by young bankers-turned-bakers. You'll find over twenty food vendors – fishmongers, butchers, greengrocers, coffee roasters, *boulangers*, *chocolatiers*, purveyors of cheese and prepared foods – many with organic, locally sourced, artisanal choices to please finicky foodies. Also in the market are clothing stalls, an art shop, candles, religious items, a barber, juice bar, snack stands, and a quirky sit-down restaurant so popular you'll wait in line for a table.

Mayor Fiorello LaGuardia opened the Essex Street Market in 1940 to eliminate thousands of pushcarts that had jammed Lower East Side streets since the turn of the century. The open-air bazaar was a social hub for the area's mostly Jewish and Italian immigrants. But it was also a nightmare scenario – streets so congested that firefighters and police often couldn't get through. LaGuardia offered pushcart peddlers the indoor retail stalls at below-market rents. In the 1950s immigrants from Puerto Rico arrived, and the area took on a *latino* flavor. Then, as now, the market's character adapted to changing tastes of its neighbors and catered to international appetites.

You can easily wile away a day exploring stalls, sampling tasty morsels, chatting with vendors that regular customers get to know on a first-name basis. One caveat: pay each seller separately. In the cluster of stands, it's often tricky to tell where one stall ends and another begins. If you absentmindedly 'travel' with an unpaid item, you'll hear loud shouts.

It's a good bet that on your way home, you'll reach into your shopping bag to gobble up some mouthwatering treats.

Address 120 Essex Street (between Delancey and Rivington Street), New York 10002, www.essexstreetmarket.com | **Transit** Subway: Essex St (J, M); Delancey St (F), Bus: M9, M14, M15, M21 | **Hours** Mon–Sat 8am–7pm, Sun 10am–6pm | **Tip** Newly-minted comedians and those you know tickle your funny-bone at Laughing Buddha Comedy Club's open mike (131 Essex Street).

39__Fanelli Cafe
The real deal

Before SoHo was SoHo, before the neighborhood got transformed into a theme park of galleries, *chi-chi* designer boutiques, and mall stores, and before 1970s artists discovered they could afford to live and work in its industrial lofts, there was Fanelli's. Located at the corner of Prince and Mercer since the day it opened in 1847, it's the second oldest food-and-drink establishment to remain in one place in New York City. What began as a workingman's ale house (with a brothel upstairs) became a hangout that watered and fed generations of factory workers, truckers, boxers, artists, and assorted guys and dolls – serving up hearty pub grub and beer on tap in an atmosphere of rough-and-tumble camaraderie.

Fanelli's deserves to be called legendary. Take a seat next to an old-timer some weekday afternoon when it's not too busy. Order a pint of draft beer and strike up a conversation. Express sincere interest and with luck you might hear tales of Prohibition in the 1920s, when Fanelli's was a local speakeasy, serving bootleg booze, wine, and beer 'distilled' in the basement. You'll learn about the man who owned it from 1922 to 1982: Mike Fanelli, a former prize-fighter who hung up photos of the boxers he admired – photos that are still on the walls – and who made it an informal clubhouse for fightfans. Order a second draft and the bartender who seemed strictly business might chime in with tales of thirsty artists and their bohemian pals who made merry in the back room in the 1970s.

Fanelli Cafe is an authentic old-school neighborhood tavern with its original long bar, tile floors, embossed tin ceilings, and wobbly tables covered with red-and-white checkered cloths. It has no Michelin star, but the burgers and sides are tasty. And while you can't order esoteric craft ales, what's on tap is frosty and satisfying. Leave fancy SoHo at the door and immerse yourself in the real deal.

Address 94 Prince Street (at Mercer Street), New York 10012, Tel +1 212.226.9412 | Transit Subway: Prince St (N, R); Broadway-Lafayette St (B, D, F, M); Bleecker St (6); Bus: M5, M21, M103 | Hours Sun–Thu 10am–1:30am, Fri–Sat 10am–4am | Tip It's a short walk to Mulberry Street, heart of Little Italy. Try world-famous cannolis and other delectable pastries at Ferrara Bakery & Cafe on Grand Street.

40_FDR Four Freedoms Park

A dream that wouldn't die

Roosevelt Island is so close to Manhattan that it'd be a short swim if not for the perilously strong currents. Instead, opt for a quick subway or aerial tram ride. Disembark on a two-mile long strip in the middle of the raging East River, notable for its dazzling views of Manhattan to the west and the borough of Queens to the east. Stroll south on the shoreline path and *voilà!* – FDR Four Freedoms Park, covering the entire southern end of the island. It's in plain sight from the city, yet few New Yorkers know about it.

Ascend the park's grand staircase and prepare for a thrill. Stretched before you is an enormous lawn bordered by elegant waterfront promenades where linden trees parade down the paths in soldier-like rows. You're mid-river with eye-popping views on all sides. While there's an air of tranquility, it's also an amazing place for a festive picnic.

At the southernmost tip, on a stark granite plaza, is a massive bronze bust of Franklin Roosevelt, gazing across the river. New York's native son, its governor, and four-term US president, he was one of the most influential figures of the twentieth century. Chiseled at the back of the monument is an inscription from his historic 1941 State of the Union address, the Four Freedoms Speech, envisioning "a world founded upon four essential freedoms." In the face of the rise of Nazism and totalitarianism, it became a rallying cry of World War II.

In 1973, celebrated architect Louis Kahn designed the commemorative park. His majestic plan paid close attention to every detail. Kahn's sudden death in 1974 stalled the project, but a fiercely determined group of prominent citizens and architects fought to keep his original concept alive. After decades of advocacy and fundraising, the park opened in 2012.

The memorial invites profound contemplation. Its spectacular river and city views are a feast for the spirit. Take time to dream.

Address 1 FDR Four Freedoms Park, Roosevelt Island, New York 10044,
Phone +1 212.204.8831, www.fdrfourfreedomspark.org | **Transit** Subway: Roosevelt Island
(F), Aerial Tram: 59 St at Second Av (once you're on the island, follow signs to walk to the
park or take a red bus that loops around the island) | **Hours** Wed–Mon 9am–5pm, closed
Tue | **Tip** The tram ride over the East River offers sky-high views. Riverfront walks reveal
surprises like Tom Otterness's whimsical in-the-water sculpture *The Marriage of Money and
Real Estate*. Stroll to the far north end to see a restored 1872 lighthouse.

I THE FUTURE DAYS WHICH WE SEEK TO MAKE SECURE
E LOOK FORWARD TO A WORLD FOUNDED UPON FOUR
SENTIAL HUMAN FREEDOMS. THE FIRST IS FREEDOM OF
PEECH AND EXPRESSION - EVERYWHERE IN THE WORLD. THE
ECOND IS FREEDOM OF EVERY PERSON TO WORSHIP GOD
HIS OWN WAY - EVERYWHERE IN THE WORLD. THE THIRD
FREEDOM FROM WANT...EVERYWHERE IN THE WORLD.
HE FOURTH IS FREEDOM FROM FEAR...ANYWHERE IN THE
ORLD. THAT IS NO VISION OF A DISTANT MILLENNIUM.
IS A DEFINITE BASIS FOR A KIND OF WORLD ATTAINABLE

41__Film Forum

Screen gems

Nothing compares with the experience of seeing a movie exactly as its director intended, in an intimate screening room with fellow film buffs. A dark theater is the ideal place to embark on a thrilling journey. Magic happens. For two or three hours, you inhabit a world projected on the screen, live in another time or place, face situations and characters you never encountered before, and walk in unfamiliar shoes.

Film Forum is NY's only autonomous nonprofit movie house. It was founded in 1970, presenting independent films in a tiny theater with just fifty folding chairs. As great art houses like the Thalia, New Yorker, and Bleecker Street Cinema closed, city filmgoers were hungry for a place to rediscover Hollywood classics and see noncommercial American and international flicks. As buzz about Film Forum spread, its following increased and it relocated, finally settling at its current site with seating for five hundred in three screening rooms.

The crowd it attracts is hip and diverse. Movie lovers rub elbows with snooty aficionados while waiting in line for fare that encompasses premieres of independent domestic and foreign art films; documentaries; US and international classics; retrospectives of directors (Hitchcock, Truffaut, Kurosawa, Woody Allen), actors (Bogey, Belmondo, Brando), and genres (B-movies, pre-code pics, apocalyptic sci-fi). Famous flops, star-studded spectacles, and obscure oddities – they're all here. Filmmakers frequently appear in person for lively post-screening Q&A sessions.

The snack bar sells popcorn (of course), also espresso and a classic chocolate egg cream. Take kids to Film Forum Jr's family-friendly Sunday morning shows. Pick up a calendar of monthly screenings and special events when you're there, or check the website. There's a good chance that you'll return often to join the audience for an astonishing wealth of silver screen treasures.

Address 209 West Houston Street (between Varick Street and Avenue of the Americas), New York 10014, Phone +1 212.727.8110, www.filmforum.org, info@filmforumnyc.org | **Transit** Subway: Houston St (1); W 4 St (A, B, C, D, E, F, M); Spring St (C, E), Bus: M5, M8, M20, M21 | **Hours** Box Office opens daily 12:15pm | **Tip** After the show, browse the huge selection of vintage and recent movie posters at Artful Posters Ltd. (194 Bleecker Street).

42__Fishing at Sheepshead Bay

Salty dogs and striped bass

Sheepshead Bay is a small fishing village on a calm inlet where ducks and swans glide. The area was named for the striped sheepshead fish, once commonly found there. In the nineteenth century, this was a genteel resort community with its own racetrack. One surviving remnant of those bygone days is the wooden footbridge that crosses the bay to Manhattan Beach.

These days, early each morning, at noon, and again in the early evening, you'll hear pier-side criers hawking fishing charters on boats with names like Sea Queen VII, Captain Dave, Ranger VI, Marilyn Jean IV, Ocean Eagle V, Flamingo III. At every dock, colorful bold-letter signs advertise prices and schedules for full-day, half-day, and evening outings. All year round, these boats head out to sea in search of daily catches that, depending on the season, include bluefish, cod, fluke, porgy, sea bass, or stripers.

Board the vessel that appeals to you and prepare to enjoy lots of fresh air and great excitement when you feel that tug on your line. Passengers are an interesting mix of regulars, frequent-fishers, and wannabe first-timers. The excursion takes you three miles out into the Atlantic, and when you reach fertile waters the captain shouts, *Drop your lines!* Then the fun begins, along with some patient waiting for a bite.

Don't expect a theme-park ride. These are working boats – many with electronic fish-finding equipment – whose captains and crews are serious about fishing, who make their living at it and earn additional income taking passengers along on trips. If you're a novice without tackle of your own, they'll provide you with rod, reel, bait, and advice on catching your dinner. They'll even clean, filet, and pack your fish.

Cruises are kid-friendly and go out whether rain or shine. Dress according to season and conditions. Snacks can be bought on board, but you're encouraged to bring your own. Anchors aweigh!

Address Emmons Avenue (between East 21st and 28th Street), Brooklyn, New York 11235 | Transit Subway: Sheepshead Bay (B, Q), Bus: B 4, B 36, B 49 | Hours Year-round daily sailings; check fishing boat websites for schedule and reservation info. | Tip After a day at sea, chow down on creamy clam chowder and sensational seafood at Randazzo's Clam Bar on 21st Street.

43_Float your boat

Waterways in the park

When the excitement of the city gets too intense, pick up a picnic lunch at the corner deli and head to The Boathouse in Central Park. Rent a rowboat and paddle out to the center of the park's scenic 22-acre woodland lake, where you can drift in harmony with puffy white clouds overhead. Beneath romantic Bow Bridge – a cast-iron beauty featured in many films, TV shows, and commercials – you're bound to spot friendly turtles who inhabit these calm waters. At the western edge of the lake is Ladies Pavilion, an elegant wrought-iron Victorian gazebo built originally as a street-trolley shelter; it was later relocated to Central Park to become a lakeside observation point and a picturesque site for weddings.

Each sturdy rowboat seats four, so you can take along family, friends, or that special someone – a perfect New York spot for a marriage proposal! – on a delicious cruise in a lush green country setting with elegant city towers lining its distant borders.

Landlubbers who prefer watching a sleek schooner or clipper ship can stroll over to the Conservatory Water on the east side of the park. Inspired by model-boat ponds in nineteenth-century European parks, this shallow oval basin is where children of all ages congregate to sail miniature wind-driven and radio-controlled vessels. All are welcome to bring their own sailboats or to rent one there. Resident 'admirals,' who return faithfully every weekend, offer navigating advice and regale you with tales of their exploits on the high seas of the pond. When your sailing day is done, venture inside the Kerbs Memorial Boathouse to see the magnificent scale-model yachts belonging to members of the Central Park Model Yacht Club. Serious model boaters, who hold much-sought-after permits, house their vessels there all year. Model yachting goes on every weekend throughout the warm months, with mini-regattas scheduled on most summer Saturdays.

Address Loeb Boathouse, mid-park at 75th Street, Phone +1 212.517.2233; Conservatory Water, between 72nd and 75th Street (near Fifth Avenue), Phone +1 212.522.0054 | Transit Subway: 72 St (B, C, 1, 2, 3); 68 St-Hunter College (6); 77 St (6), Bus: M1, M2, M3, M4, M72 | Hours Loeb Boathouse: Apr.–Oct. daily 10am–5:30pm; Conservatory Water Apr.–Oct. Mon–Thu 11am–7pm, Fri 11am–10pm, Sat 1–10pm, Sun 10am–8pm | Tip West of the pond on summer Saturdays, kids flock to 11am story hour at the Hans Christian Anderson statue. To its north, youngsters year-round climb all over the whimsical Alice in Wonderland statue.

44_Flying Lessons
With no wings attached

What could be more exhilarating than a view of the Freedom Tower and the Statue of Liberty as you fly on a trapeze – heart racing and *upside down* – high above Hudson River Park at Pier 40!

If you're new to the trapeze, sign up for the beginner's class. In a group of ten first-timers, you join an adventurous mix of daring (and nervous) tourists and native New Yorkers – birthday celebrants, dating couples, adrenaline freaks, folks confronting their phobias, and daredevil kids bored with tame playgrounds.

With shoes off and chalk on your hands, you climb a narrow metal ladder to a platform 23-feet high, where an instructor awaits and readies you for takeoff. Despite safety nets and a harness around your waist attached to ropes held by instructors on the ground, it's still scary. Fear and trembling are common. Skilled in the art of encouragement, your instructor coaxes you to "lean hips-forward at a ten-degree angle," grab the heavier-than-you'd-imagine trapeze bar with one hand, then the other, and take that unforgettable first leap. *Whee!*

You'll get four or five chances to fly – with ground-level coaching between flights. By the time the two-hour class ends, you've mastered the knee-hang and backflip, and even had a chance to be caught mid-air by an instructor!

Don't be surprised to see shirt-and-tie corporate types flying high at lunch hour – it's utilized as a powerful team-building activity. Celebrities are also captivated by this exciting, super-scenic experience. Trapeze School New York has been featured on TV shows like *Sex and the City* and *Modern Family*, and Hugh Jackman took trapeze lessons here to train for his *Wolverine* role!

Equally thrilling is TSNY's East River location, beside the historic tall ships at South Street Seaport's Pier 16. Either location affords breathtaking day and night skyline views – and a sensational opportunity to defy gravity.

Address a) Pier 40, 353 West Street (between West Houston and Clarkson Street), New York 10014; b) Pier 16, South Street (at Fulton Street), New York 10038, Phone +1 917.797.1872, www.newyork.trapezeschool.com, info@trapezeschool.com | Transit a) Subway: Houston St (1), Bus: M 8, M 20, M 21; b) Subway: Fulton St (2, 3, J, Z), Bus: M 15 | Hours May–Oct. daily 10am–10:30pm | Tip Hudson River Park's wide, well-tended running and cycling paths and spacious lawns afford sensational riverside and harbor views.

45 — Ford Foundation Atrium

A refuge from the urban jungle

It's an attractive glass-and-steel mid-century office building. Manhattan has many. But this is no ordinary building, and its lobby is no ordinary lobby.

Step into the Ford Foundation's headquarters and all at once you're far from urban life, inside a lush, whisper-quiet tropical forest. You're transported into a romantic setting, enclosed by a ten-story-high atrium filled with bright natural light and exquisitely landscaped paths that gently wind through terraced plantings, tall trees, and a reflecting pool. Although you're enveloped within a tower, the scale is human, the experience is unique. Usually, you'll see no one. Except for the softly bubbling water, this is a silent sanctum. It's hard to imagine you're in a place where lots of people are busy working.

The garden at the center of the Ford Foundation Building is an important component of a forward-thinking concept developed in the 1960s by architects Kevin Roche and John Dinkeloo. With a powerful appreciation of the Foundation's philanthropic mission of advancing human welfare, their design reflected a deep concern for its employees, fostering an environment of collaboration and community. Instead of workspaces facing outward to the frenetic city, the offices and conference rooms in this building were turned outside-in, and were made see-through so workers would be visible to one another across the atrium and could overlook the serene woodland retreat at its core. The urban greenspace idea became a model for other workplaces and modern indoor shopping malls.

A socio-architectural masterpiece that won landmark status in 1997, it is also one of the first environmentally sensitive "green" buildings in the city. It was designed so its glass south wall retains solar heat; rainwater collected on the roof fills its pool and irrigates plantings; and maximal use of natural light saves energy.

Stop by to escape and refresh.

Address 320 East 43rd Street (between Tudor City Place and Second Avenue), New York 10017, Phone +1 212.573.5000, www.fordfoundation.org | Transit Subway: Grand Central-42 St (4, 5, 6, 7, S), Bus: M 15, M 42, M 101, M 102, M 103 | Hours Mon−Fri 10am−4pm | Tip Discover the lobby garden at Japan Society (333 East 47th Street), a museum and cultural center celebrating Japanese history, arts, language.

46 Fragrance Garden
Indulge in sense-sational delights

The most pleasantly odoriferous attraction in Brooklyn challenges you to get up-close and personal with plants. Most public gardens enforce a strict look-but-don't-touch policy, but in the Fragrance Garden at the Brooklyn Botanic Garden you're expected to break established rules. Here you are encouraged to handle leaves and petals, stroke them, break off pieces, and vigorously rub them between your fingers to experience an extraordinary variety of aromatic and tactile sensations.

Although originally conceived in 1955 by landscape architect Alice Recknagel Ireys as a specialty garden for the blind and sight-impaired – with flowerbed labels and signs in braille – this stunning garden-within-the-Garden is a source of great enjoyment for visitors young and old, blind and sighted.

At its center is a neatly manicured oval lawn, encircled by a wide flagstone walkway. All around the perimeter of this path, elevated planting beds – at a level comfortably accessible to both wheelchairs and small children – display a medley of horticultural specimens. These are arranged in four groups based upon the way each tickles the senses. Plants that excite touch vary in texture from soft, smooth lamb's ears to sharp, prickly agave. When you rub the leaves of a scented-leaf group (lavender, patchouli, sage, lemon verbena) or the abundant kitchen herbs (basil, sweet marjoram, spearmint, dill, rosemary) and then smell your fingertips, the result can be intoxicating. And deep whiffs of fragrant flowers like sweet alyssum, flowering tobacco, and evening primrose might make you swoon.

After you've completed the entire circuit, take a seat on one of the benches along the path and engage another one of your senses. You'll hear the sound of birds in the trees accompanied by exclamations of surprise *(Wow! Did you smell this one?)*, and the gleeful laughter of children.

Address Entrances at 150 Eastern Parkway and 990 Washington Avenue (at Classon Avenue), Brooklyn, New York 11225, Phone +1 718.623.7200, www.bbg.org, info@bbg.org | **Transit** Subway: Eastern Pkwy-Brooklyn Museum (2, 3); Franklin Av (4, 5); Prospect Park (B, Q), Bus: B 16, B 41, B 43, B 45, B 48, B 49 | **Hours** Fragrance Garden is open mid-June to mid-Sep. Tue – Fri 8am – 6pm and Sat – Sun 10am – 6pm | **Tip** Inside Brooklyn Botanic, explore adjacent Shakespeare Garden, then stroll Celebrity Path inscribed with names of famous Brooklynites.

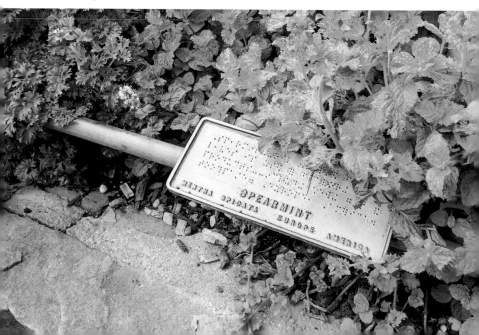

47__Gertrude Stein Statue
Buddha in Bryant Park

Seated on a marble pedestal on the upper terrace of Bryant Park – the tree-lined backyard of the New York Public Library's landmark Beaux Arts building – is a statue of Gertrude Stein, an extraordinary author whose writings defied literary tradition, who collected groundbreaking art, and who mentored and challenged the avant-garde writers, artists, and musicians of the 1920s. Its location, a few steps from the city's monumental shrine to books and ideas, pays tribute to her importance to modernism and the life of the mind.

Seasonal transformations of the park for holiday craft bazaars, ice skating, and concerts might make her hard to find, but once spotted, she'll remain forever in your memory. This seated figure is less than 3 feet tall, yet she seems larger than life – contemplative, heavy-set, sitting cross-legged with a long skirt draped over her knees, she embodies earthiness and strength. Sculptor Jo Davidson attended Stein's fabled Saturday evening salons at 27 Rue de Fleurus in Paris, where the likes of Hemingway, Joyce, Fitzgerald, Picasso, and Matisse rubbed elbows to discuss and often shatter conventional ideas about art and life. Davidson, who persuaded Stein to pose for him in 1920, remarked, "To do a head of Gertrude was not enough – there was so much more to her than that. So I did a seated figure of her – a sort of modern Buddha." When the statue was unveiled in 1923, critics called it ugly, unflattering. Gertrude reportedly loved it.

The bronze casting in Bryant Park is eighth in a series of ten made from the original – two others are in the collections of New York's Whitney and Metropolitan Museums. You may be astonished to learn that this statue, donated to the newly refurbished Bryant Park in 1992 by prominent New York art dealer and psychologist, Dr. Maury Leibovitz, became the first sculpture of an American woman ever to be installed in a New York City park.

Address Enter at West 40th Street and Fifth Avenue. Statue is at southeast end of Bryant Park's upper terrace, behind New York Public Library. | Transit Subway: 42 St-Bryant Pk (B, D, F, M); 5 Av (7), Bus: M 1, M 2, M 3, M 4, M 5, M 42 | Tip The beloved Library Lions were named Patience and Fortitude by Mayor Fiorello LaGuardia. Find all NYC Parks Department monuments online: www.nycgovparks.org/art-and-antiquities/permanent-art-and-monuments.

48__ The Gospel Truth
Sunday services in Harlem

It's no secret that many of today's R&B, soul, and hip hop stars first raised their voices in church, singing in a gospel choir. Harlem's churches are vital centers of social and spiritual life where members of close-knit congregations – primarily African-American – assemble in their Sunday-best attire to greet each other, worship, listen to sermons, and join together in song. Choral music at many of these services is so dynamic, it's become a popular tourist attraction. Parishioners at some of the bigger churches often wince when their houses of worship are jammed with tourists eager to 'see a show.'

An exception is Convent Avenue Baptist Church, home to one of the most welcoming congregations in Harlem. Come on any Sunday just before the 8am or 11am service, and an usher dressed in white greets you with friendly conversation and hands you the morning's program, with pamphlets (printed in several languages) describing the church and its mission. Many churches ask visitors to sit in a designated area, but Convent Avenue Baptist not only invites you to take a seat wherever you like, but devotes a portion of the service to welcoming all newcomers, asking them to stand and be greeted by the full congregation.

Music is so integral to worship here that a vital member of its clergy is its Minister of Music. In a choir loft facing the congregation directly above the altar, Convent Avenue's renowned chorus offers "praise through song," featuring traditional hymns and raise-the-roof gospel music that lift the spirit of worshippers who joyfully sing along. The service lasts for two hours, with extraordinary vocals underscoring and connecting the program of prayer, readings from scripture, a pastoral talk, calls for offerings, and a heartfelt sermon.

In an inspirational setting, here's an uplifting way to begin your Sunday – with a taste of what might best be described as pure soul food.

Address 420 West 145th Street (between Convent and St Nicholas Avenue), New York 10031, **Phone** +1 646.698.5100, www.conventchurch.org, contactcabc@conventchurch.org | **Transit Subway:** 145 St (A, B, C, D, 1), Bus: M 3, M 4, M 5, M 10, M 100, M 101 | **Hours** Sun 8am and 11am | **Tip** Stroll the leafy campus of City College (Convent Avenue, 130th to 141st Street), alma mater of 10 Nobel Prize winners.

49 __ Governors Island
Not that far from the madding crowd

It is so close to Brooklyn that farmers used to walk their cows across Buttermilk Channel to graze there until it was dredged shipping-lane deep. Used for military purpose for the next few hundred years, the island oasis has only recently been made available for recreational use.

The Dutch bought what was a fishing camp from the Lenape tribe in 1637 for two ax heads, a string of beads, and some nails. In 1784 Britain claimed it to accommodate "His Majesties Governors," hence the name.

Its history as a military outpost is varied. After the American Revolution, an inner-harbor defense network was created to protect New York from naval attack. Its fort repelled the British navy in the War of 1812. It was a Civil War prison. In WWII it housed strategists of the D-Day Normandy landing. From 1966-96 it was the largest US Coast Guard base in the world, with 3,500 residents living a small-town life a stone's throw from America's largest city. In 2001 the government designated 22 acres as Governors Island National Monument, and in 2003 the remainder of the island was sold to the people of NY.

Now, a quick ferry ride from either Manhattan or Brooklyn transports you to this reinvented mid-harbor playground. It's carefree and car-free. You can be active: ride a bike (bring your own or rent one there), paddle a kayak, fly a kite. Or be lazy: lounge in a shady grove of hammocks, picnic, watch the boats float by. Enjoy a tempting array of city-hosted activities: art events, concerts, performances, workshops, culinary extravaganzas, and themed festivals like the Jazz Age Lawn Party where Gatsby-era dress is *de rigueur*. And did we mention the view?

Dutch landscape architects (what goes around comes around!) are now developing the island with green, sustainable designs to include pastures and hilly parklands. So bring sunscreen, comfy shoes, and a spirit of adventure.

Address Manhattan Ferry: Battery Maritime Building, 10 South Street (at Whitehall Street), New York 10004; Brooklyn Ferry: Brooklyn Bridge Park, Pier 6 (south end of park), www.govisland.com, info@govisland.nyc.gov | **Transit** for Manhattan Ferry: Subway: South Ferry (1); Bowling Green (4, 5); Whitehall St (N, R); Broad St (J, Z), Bus: M 5, M 15, M 20; for Brooklyn Ferry: Subway: High St (A, C); York St (F); Clark St (2, 3); Court St (R), Bus: B 25, B 61, B 63, B 67 | **Hours** Late May – late Sep. Mon – Fri 10am – 6pm, Sat – Sun 10am – 7pm | **Tip** The Downtown Connection is a *free bus* making 37 stops (including State and Whitehall Streets near the ferry) between South Street Seaport and Battery Park City (www.downtowny.com/getting-around/downtown-connection).

50__Grate sound
Times Square humdinger

A peculiar sound floats up through a metal grate in the sidewalk of one of Times Square's busiest intersections. Garish neon lights pulse and flash, enormous billboards compete for attention, and wildly animated colorful images crawl over every surface. Here, amid the cacophony of blaring traffic, rushing crowds, beeping horns, and shouting vendors – a high-decibel area if there ever was one – the bizarre sound that rises through this iron grid is clear and distinct. Some call it a persistent hum, others compare it with a faraway reverberating gong. More musical than a vibration, mellower than a buzz, its sustained single note almost sounds like the sacred chanted syllable, *Om*.

Head over to the 46th Street end of the triangular pedestrian island between Broadway and Seventh Avenue, where costumed characters like Elmo and Statue-of-Liberty Man like to hang out. If you stand near the grate you won't need to lean down or strain your ears. Just listen – it's unmistakable. *Omm, humm ...* While hordes of people tread across this same spot day and night, almost no one appears to notice it. If they detect it at all, they may assume it's nearby construction in a subway tunnel.

But, in fact, it's a very deliberate installation of auditory art created in 1977 by the late artist-in-sound Max Neuhaus, who expected that most people would walk by without paying any attention to it. He hoped certain others would encounter it, stop for a moment to experience its indescribable mechanical drone, and be surprised by the revelation. And because Neuhaus specified that no sign be posted to identify or explain its existence, you have no way to know it's there at all! For a decade, 1992-2002, it was removed by the artist, but later reinstalled by the Dia Art Foundation. Today, this strangely haunting hum continues to escape from the belly of the beast that is Times Square – day after day, year after year.

Address North side of triangular pedestrian island between West 45th and 46th Street and between Broadway and Seventh Avenue | Transit Subway: Times Sq-42 St (N, Q, R, S, 1, 2, 3, 7); 49 St (N, Q, R), Bus: M 5, M 7, M 20, M 42, M 50, M 104 | Hours 24/7 |

Tip Pounding sounds and pulsating rhythms reverberate amidst a vast array of genuine rock memorabilia at the Hard Rock Cafe (1501 Broadway).

51 Greenwich Locksmiths
Captivated by keys

From a distance, this West Village storefront appears unevenly painted in brownish-gray tones. A closer look at the facade of the lilliputian locksmith shop, scarcely bigger than a newsstand, reveals something amazing. Covering every exterior surface of the storefront are exquisitely-crafted patterned mosaics composed entirely of ... keys!

Ordinary household keys are ingeniously welded into stunning works of art. The swirling, undulating, spiraling, and circular designs are the work of Philip Mortillaro, the shop's owner, chief locksmith, and a Village institution. Sit on the key-encrusted metal chair beside the entrance and you'll observe a steady stream of people coming in to copy a key and schmooze, swap stories, discuss and debate news with the *key-meister* – a neighborhood raconteur, political pundit, philosopher, and trusted friend.

At fourteen, Phil took a summer job sorting key blanks for a midtown locksmith. His early fascination with keys and locks led to an apprenticeship and a lifelong passion for the art of locksmithing. He opened his first shop on Union Square in 1969, then in 1980 moved to the current location. The idea of embellishing its storefront with keys – first the door, then the chair, and finally the entire facade – was a natural outgrowth of Phil's talent for welding and creative metalwork. Thousands of keys culled from a scrap-metal firm comprise the shop's remarkable exterior. Over time, every surface has weathered to a rich patina and an intricate sculptural beauty. Interior walls are lined with thousands of keys and locks, some centuries old, many odd or unusual, and each with a story Phil loves to tell. History embedded in hardware is what's most fascinating to him.

Behind the counter, in the narrow V-shaped space that can barely fit two, you'll find Phil and his dedicated son – the young man to whom, one day, he plans to hand over the keys.

Address 56 Seventh Avenue South, (between Morton and Commerce Street), NY 10014,
Phone +1 212.242.4646, www.greenwichlocksmiths.com | Transit Subway: Christopher
St/Sheridan Sq (1); West 4th St (A, B, C, D, E, F, M), Bus: M8, M11, M12, M14A, M20,
M21 | Hours Mon–Fri 8:30am–6pm | Tip World-famous jazz musicians never play
off-key at the Village Vanguard (178 Seventh Avenue South), a popular Greenwich Village
'scene' since 1935.

52 __ Green-Wood Cemetery
Heaven here on earth

Pass through the fairytale Gothic Revival main gate. Ahead, in all directions, are 478 acres of rolling hills, valleys, lily ponds, and wooded paths extending as far as you can see. You wonder where to begin, which way to walk, and if your legs are up to exploring its vast expanse.

Head for the Visitors Center. Unless you're in the market for a burial plot (which the affable staff can readily sell you) they'll assist you in navigating the grounds. Using a map of the site, they'll suggest routes tailored to your interests, pinpointing historic and contemporary gravesites, memorials, and works of art. Whether you're a history buff, art lover, birdwatcher, or seek a tranquil space to ponder and daydream, you're bound to derive pleasure from the elysian landscape.

When it was founded in 1838, Green-Wood was not just the most fashionable burial place for the elite but also a wildly popular nineteenth-century tourist destination – incredibly, it was second only to Niagara Falls! Decades before the creation of Central Park, Prospect Park, or the Metropolitan Museum of Art, this was both a bucolic recreational oasis and an open-air sculpture garden. Today it's all that and a historical museum as well.

The roster of 'residents' in this idyllic memorial park is impressive. Here lie heroes, rogues, soldiers, sports legends, politicians, artists, entertainers, and inventors alongside ordinary citizens. It's fun to search out the famous and the infamous. Consult your map for the final resting places of Peter Cooper, Henry Ward Beecher, Elias Howe, DeWitt Clinton, Louis Comfort Tiffany, several of the Roosevelts, Lola Montez, Leonard Bernstein, Jean-Michel Basquiat. Then climb to the top of Battle Hill, a Revolutionary War site and the highest point in Brooklyn, to the austere statue of the robed and helmeted goddess Minerva. She stares across the river at the Statue of Liberty. From Heaven.

Address 500 25th Street (at 5th Avenue), Brooklyn, New York 11232,
Phone +1 718.768.7300, www.greenwoodcemetery.org | Transit Subway: 25 St (D, N, R);
36 St (D, N, R), Bus: B 63 | Hours Main Entrance (25th Street): Winter: daily 8am – 5pm,
Spring: daily 8am – 6pm, Summer: daily 8am – 7pm; Side Entrance (4th Avenue): Sat – Sun
8am – 4pm | Tip Stop at nearby Sea Witch Tavern on 5th Avenue for their celebrated craft
brews and pub food. Reliable sources claim that Sea Witch conducts cool unofficial and
unorthodox tours of Green-Wood (seawitchnyc.com).

53__Hall of Fame for Great Americans

Big men and women on campus

Perched on one of the highest points in the Bronx, with postcard views of the Harlem River, Manhattan, and the distant New Jersey Palisades, is the Hall of Fame for Great Americans – a semicircular, 630-foot-long, open-air colonnade. Set between its neo-classical columns are bronze busts of noteworthy Americans: statesmen, soldiers, scientists, educators, humanitarians, inventors, theologians, authors, artists, musicians, and actors whose impact on the nation's history has been significant. Staring right at you – deliberately designed to return your gaze – are the likes of Abraham Lincoln, Booker T. Washington, Mark Twain, and Susan B. Anthony. The busts represent the most important collection of bronze portraiture in the US.

Designed by premier architect Stanford White on what was then NYU's campus, this national shrine was dedicated in 1901 and quickly became a popular tourist attraction. There are ninety-eight notables on display and four awaiting placement. Typical of its era, honorees were mostly male and white; eleven are women and two are African-American. They each have a plaque – many crafted by Tiffany – inscribed with their name, significant dates, achievements, and an apt quotation.

As the first hall of fame in America, it was precursor to all that followed. During the active selection process (1900 to 1973), citizens could submit nominations to an electors committee of illustrious Americans. For many years, induction to this venerated roster carried more weight in social and intellectual circles than that of Nobel laureate.

Bronx Community College bought the campus from NYU in 1973 and sadly the Hall's renown began to fade. Today, few New Yorkers are aware of the existence of this majestic promenade.

It's still amazing. Take a docent-led tour for a surprising and beautiful walk through the annals of American history.

Address Hall of Fame Terrace at Bronx Community College, 2155 University Avenue (between West 180th and 181st Street), Bronx, New York 10453, Phone +1 718.289.5180 (to schedule a tour), www.bcc.cuny.edu/halloffame | Transit Subway: Burnside Av (4), Bus: BX 3, BX 32, BX 40, BX 42 | Hours Daily 10am–5pm | Tip On campus, Stanford White's Gould Memorial Library has a splendid Pantheon-inspired domed space with rare Connemara green marble columns and Tiffany stained glass windows.

MIGHTY MEN WHICH WERE OF OLD · MEN OF RENOWN

54 — Hangman's Tree
Swinging in Washington Square

If trees could talk, the English elm at the northwest corner of Washington Square Park would have fascinating, spine-chilling tales to tell. Giant-sized – 110 feet high with a trunk five feet thick – it's thought to be Manhattan's oldest living tree, witness to three centuries of NYC history. Although chroniclers of the park's past have discovered no official record of hangings on these wide boughs, it has nevertheless long been known as Hangman's Tree. Legends describing its horrific past emerged and, over the years, grew increasingly detailed, often plausible. Like claims that during the Revolutionary War, traitors were hanged from this tree and then buried in the adjacent potter's field where Indians, slaves, paupers, and victims of epidemics were interred. Or that condemned inmates from nearby Newgate Prison dangled from its branches when death sentences were carried out.

The only *documented* execution to take place here was that of Rose Butler, a slave convicted of setting fire to her master's home. She was hanged – but not from this tree – in 1820, when gallows stood at the site of the present-day arch. A hangman-gravedigger, residing in a nearby shack, performed public executions on Sunday mornings, burials in the afternoon.

Converted to a park in 1827, Washington Square today is unofficially NYU's campus quad. This city icon was a sixties mecca for flower children (immortalized in *Hair*), spawned music legends like Bob Dylan and Buddy Holly, and is historically a political activism arena. The beloved green space attracts locals and visitors, aspiring musicians and acrobats, cuddling couples. Stroll past Hangman's Tree by day to encounter players at chess tables, kids splashing in the fountain, profs off to class, dog-walkers on a stroll. But at night, according to legend, ghosts of souls buried below emerge from their graves to cavort and swing from the branches.

Address Northwest corner of Washington Square Park, Washington Square North (at Macdougal Street), New York 10011 | **Transit** Subway: W 4 St (A, B, C, D, E, F, M); Christopher St-Sheridan Sq (1); 8 St-NYU (N, R); Astor Pl (6), Bus: M 1, M 2, M 3, M 5, M 8, M 20 | **Tip** Marshall Chess Club (23 West 10th Street) was the site of 13-year-old Bobby Fisher's victorious "Game of the Century" in 1956.

55 Harriet Tubman's Skirt
Towering freedom fighter

The Harriet Tubman statue, *Swing Low*, has been described as a moving train in the form of a woman, arms like pumping pistons, her exposed underskirt suggesting a cowcatcher (the grill mounted on a locomotive to clear obstacles in its path). Nothing could derail this figure from her journey; her strong features gaze straight ahead, unblinking and purposeful. Breaking free of the thick, tangled roots of bondage, she leaves behind remnants of a brutal past and its baggage. Emerging from the surface of her skirt are faces of escaped slaves, worn-out soles of their shoes, and other symbols of captivity – shackles, chains, iron keys. The monument is a painful reminder of racial oppression, and a tribute to Tubman's lifelong commitment to the cause.

Araminta Ross was born into slavery in 1820s Maryland. Escaping in 1849, she navigated the Underground Railroad – not an actual railway, but a secret network of routes and safe-houses providing runaway slaves a means of escape to freedom. In Philadelphia she became an abolitionist, changed her name to Harriet Tubman to conceal her identity, and went back and forth to the plantations, leading hundreds of slaves to freedom. They called her their Moses.

During the Civil War, Tubman served as a nurse and spy for the Union army. In 1863, she planned and led a river raid in South Carolina resulting in a military triumph and liberation of nearly eight hundred slaves. After the war, she dedicated herself to the cause of racial equality, the rights of women, the poor, disabled, and underserved.

Swing Low stands tall at a crossroad in Harlem. The statue was installed facing south. When some locals objected, demanding she be turned to face north (symbolically toward freedom), its African-American sculptor, Alison Saar, insisted she not be moved. It was on Tubman's travels south that she heroically risked her own freedom and life to rescue others.

Address West 122nd Street (at St. Nicholas Avenue and Frederick Douglass Boulevard), New York 10027 | Transit Subway: 125 St (A, B, C, D), Bus: M 2, M 3, M 7, M 10, M 11, M 100, M 101, M 104, M 116 | Tip Find traditional African textiles, handicrafts, jewelry, art, and one-of-a-kind clothing at Malcolm Shabazz Market (52 West 116th Street), an exciting outdoor marketplace.

56 __ Henderson Place

A secret street

Tucked away on the eastern border of Yorkville is a storybook cul-de-sac where nineteenth-century Queen Anne townhouses nestle beneath high-rise luxury towers. Each house on this quiet lane is uniquely designed. Elizabethan, Flemish, and classical details adorn their entrances with multi-paned windows, arches, dormers – and, turning the corner onto East End Avenue, marvelous chimneys, turrets, gables, and oriels. The charm and dignity of the street offers a welcome stroll through simpler times.

When it was first settled by early German immigrants, Yorkville was five miles north of the city's bustle – a rural district where wealthy merchants like John Jacob Astor and Archibald Gracie owned elegant farms and riverside estates. When New York Central Railroad reached uptown, the area became attractive to titans of industry who relocated there, erecting extravagant limestone mansions along its leafy boulevards. As industry moved in, factories and tenement buildings sprang up near the river, altering the area's class structure. Businessman John Henderson, seeing an opportunity to develop private residences for "persons of moderate means" who looked to escape the crowded city, purchased a small parcel of land between York and East End Avenues. He hired Lamb & Rich (architects of Teddy Roosevelt's Long Island estate), and the Henderson Houses were completed in 1882. Their three-story height was shorter and interiors more compact than the grander townhouses, yet these picturesque homes became sought-after dwellings for generations of New Yorkers. Over the years, they have attracted well-known and well-heeled residents, including a French duke and duchess and the famous American theater couple, Lunt & Fontanne.

Of its thirty-two original houses, twenty-four have survived — intact and beautifully preserved. After so many decades, Henderson Place remains a hidden gem and a highly desirable address.

Address East 86th Street (between York and East End Avenue), New York 10028 |
Transit Subway: 86 St (4, 5, 6), Bus: M 15, M 31, M 86, M 101, M 102, M 103 | Tip Across
East End Avenue is Gracie Mansion, a 1799 wood-frame house and the official residence
of New York City's mayor since 1942. Public tours are conducted on Wednesdays
(gracie-tours@cityhall.nyc.gov).

57 __ The High Road to a Tibetan Retreat

Elevate your spirits

It's appropriate that your visit to a haven for Tibetan art begins with a trek. Take a train to a ferry, then a bus, then climb a steep, curving path up a hill. This rustic retreat has been called 'Shangri-La in Staten Island,' but you won't need a Sherpa to reach it – just sensible shoes.

Jacques Marchais moved to Staten Island in 1921. She was an unusual woman-with-a-man's-name, an actress and iconoclast interested in spiritualism and Buddhism. When her fascination for Tibet evolved into a consuming passion, Marchais began a life-long study of Tibetan culture and art. Some considered her an eccentric, but her fascination was serious and scholarly. Although she never traveled there, she became an expert, amassing an important research library and one of the most extensive collections of Tibetan art outside of Tibet.

Opened in 1947 as the Jacques Marchais Museum of Tibetan Art, its building and grounds were designed by Marchais to resemble a Himalayan monastery with a chanting-hall gallery space, library, two meditation cells, terraced gardens, and a goldfish and lotus pond. The serenity of the grounds makes you glad you came, and the collection of rare and sacred artifacts rewards you with a spiritual experience. While it's not a dharma center or religious institution, in 1991 the Dalai Lama visited and remarked on its authenticity.

Between tall, elaborately decorated columns in the rock-walled gallery are row upon row of bronze figures (all shapes and sizes, some draped with silk) of the Buddha and his avatars. Next to them are exquisite turquoise-blue enameled urns, vases, incense burners, and stoves. Walk around the room to discover rare treasure and marvel at the carved chests, furniture, ritual knives, textiles, and altarpieces.

Bring along lunch, linger at a stone table, and meditate on a rocky ledge beneath the trees.

Address 338 Lighthouse Avenue, Staten Island, New York 10306, Phone +1 718.987.3500, www.tibetanmuseum.org, info@tibetanmuseum.org | **Transit** to Staten Island Ferry: Subway: South Ferry (1); Bowling Green (4, 5); Whitehall St-South Ferry (R), Bus: M5, M15, M20; from ferry terminal in Staten Island: Bus: S74 (to Lighthouse Avenue) | **Hours** Wed – Sun 1 – 5pm (call to confirm winter hours) | **Tip** Historic Richmond Town, a living history museum complex, is three blocks from the bus stop at the base of Lighthouse Hill.

58_Hua Mei Birds
Sweetly tweeted symphonies

Early every morning, rain or shine, you'll hear them before you see them – exotic birds in a leafy enclave south of Delancey Street, between Chrystie and Forsyth, warbling melodies so enchanting they eclipse the noisy commotion of city streets.

Hua Mei Bird Garden is a small fenced-off area in Sara Delano Roosevelt Park where members of the Hua Mei Bird Club – elderly Chinese men from all walks of life who are passionate about songbirds – bring their feathered friends for fresh air and the chance to perfect their songs beside other birds. Cages sit on the ground and hang from trees, poles, or pipes. White cotton covers shielding them from city noise are slowly pulled back, birds awaken, and sweet rhapsodies fill the air.

An outsider might view this as an entertaining pastime for doddering old men, but it's actually a serious, labor-intensive, and expensive hobby. While you may see a finch or chickadee, most of them are authentic Hua Mei birds, song thrushes indigenous to China and Vietnam. They cost hundreds, and sometimes thousands, of dollars to acquire, depending on their physical attributes. A required month-long quarantine before they may enter the US costs hundreds more. Once these precious birds clear customs, they're enthroned in handmade bamboo cages fitted out with hand-painted porcelain feeding cups. A lengthy process of nurture and training follows, ensuring that they (and their owners) can successfully compete at the Hua Mei Bird Garden.

Club members commune there every day, but on weekends you'll see and hear the greatest number of men and birds. Friendly rivalry in judging cages, porcelain cups, plumage, overall beauty, and especially song virtuosity can be fierce. It is said that each bird's unique song changes when it hears those of other birds. In concert, these winged virtuosos produce beautifully intricate, melodic patterns. And the result is pure magic!

Address Sara Delano Roosevelt Park, Delancey Street (between Forsyth and Chrystie Street), New York 10002 | Transit Subway: 2 Av (F); Bowery (J, Z); Delancey St-Essex St (J, F, M); Grand St (B, D), Bus: M 9, M 14A, M 15, M 21, M 22, M 103 | Hours Daily 7am – noon | Tip Catch a first-run art film at Landmark Sunshine Theater – built in 1909 as a Yiddish vaudeville theater, the Houston Hippodrome.

59__Indoor Extreme Sports
Be the game

Get off the couch. Make a beeline to Indoor Extreme Sports and immerse yourself in an adrenaline-pumping world of thrilling interactive games. The moment you enter the outer staging area you'll feel an energy surge. Ahead of you lies an intense physical and mental workout – guys and gals, all ages and descriptions, can't wait to get inside and let loose.

Follow the screams of ecstatic players into the cavernous 34,000-square-foot fantasy space, divided into distinct arenas designed for adventure-play, that literally bombards your senses, tests your reflexes, and awakens your reptilian brain.

Choose from various games: ReBall is a reinvention of paintball, delivering the pain without the paint. In Archery Tag (a *Hunger Games*-type scenario), teams scramble to grab bows and foam-tipped arrows, then race past barricades to overtake one another. Black Ops Laser Tag equips you with gear replicating the look and feel of authentic military attire and rifles. Combat-team members stage a raid through a landscape of realistic trees, barrels, and smoke-filled booby traps. It's hi-tech – your vest lights up red and your gun stops working if you get shot.

The most heart-stopping game of all is Friday night's Zombie Experience. Armed with laser guns, join a small group of jittery explorers to navigate a vast black-light labyrinth filled with the walking living dead! You're forewarned that these zombies (professional actors hired to act really terrifying) will poke, push, menace, even slobber on you. It's so scary you're given a 'safe word' in case you freak out. Every two months the maze is reconfigured to keep it fresh for repeaters. It's so popular – reservations recommended!

Perfect for parties, team-building events, or just plain fun with pals, Indoor Extreme Sports delivers. Kids can't get enough of the excitement. And even if you're not a kid, it'll make you feel like one all over again.

Address 47–11 Van Dam Street (between 47th and 48th Avenue), Queens, New York 11101, **Phone** +1 718.361.9152, www.indoorextremesports.com, info@indoorextremesports.com | **Transit** Subway: 33 St-Rawson St (7), Bus: Q32, Q39, Q60, Q67 | **Hours** Tue–Thu 1–11pm, Fri 1pm–1am, Sat 10am–1am, Sun 10am–8pm | **Tip** Local #7 train stops at nearby ethnic neighborhoods (Sunnyside, Woodside, Jackson Heights, Corona, Flushing) whose restaurants offer authentic cuisines at modest prices.

60__Irish Hunger Memorial
The persistence of memory

In the shade of the Freedom Tower, below the financial district's sky-scraping shrines to wealth and plenty, sits a compelling monument to a million Irish men, women, and children who died of hunger in *An Gorta Mor* – the Great Potato Famine of 1845-52 – and another million forced by starvation to emigrate to the US. Through the lens of this catastrophic event, the Irish Hunger Memorial addresses the calamity of hunger and displacement in today's world.

Created by artist Brian Tolle for Battery Park City Conservancy, it is both public art and a profound experience. Enter at street level through a dimly lit corridor striped with glass and Kilkenny limestone engraved with writings reflecting the horrors of famine. Overhead, recorded voices talk about hunger and mingle with mournful Irish melodies. Emerge from the tunnel and you're outside amid the crumbled ruins of a stone cottage that once stood in County Mayo. Countless starving families abandoned homes like this all over Ireland in desperate search of food. Open to the sky, its thatched roof and mud walls were destroyed, rendering it unlivable to any who might think to return.

Your spirits lift as you walk the country path that meanders up a rising meadowed parapet, jutting high above the riverside promenade. Planted with grasses, shrubs, and flowers native to the Emerald Isle, it's a wildly beautiful place that invites contemplation. On the meadow and along the trail are 32 inscribed stones, each donated to the site from the Irish county bearing its name. At the top of the hilly path, the grassy overlook faces the Statue of Liberty and Ellis Island – an inspiring sight that gave renewed hope to the famished immigrants as they entered the harbor.

This "piece of the old sod" in New York City and the tragedy it commemorates encourages us to reflect on the disastrous consequences of worldwide hunger and to respond with action.

Address 290 Vesey Street (at North End Avenue), New York 10282, Phone +1 212.267.9700, www.nycgovparks.org/video/179 | Transit Subway: Fulton St (4, 5); Chambers St (1, A, C); Chambers St (2, 3); World Trade Center (E); City Hall (R), Bus: M 9, M 20, M 22 | Hours Daily 11:30am – 6:30pm | Tip To immerse yourself in the immigrant experience, take a ferry to the Ellis Island Immigration Museum. From there you'll get spectacular views of the city skyline. Boats depart from Battery Park daily 9am – 5pm.

61 Jane's Carousel
A real survivor

In a classic rags-to-riches tale, what was once a Midwestern carnival ride is now an urban treasure on the Brooklyn waterfront, housed in a transparent jewel-box pavilion designed by noted French architect Jean Nouvel. Art and magic combine when you ride one of the 48 painted ponies alongside a posse of giddy-up kids and hand-holding couples.

Like many New Yorkers, Jane's Carousel was born someplace else, moved here, and after a time found its heart and home in this city. Like other New York transplants, it arrived with a fascinating history, distinctive character, and that special something that tests the mettle of newcomers.

This story begins in 1922 when the carousel was built for an amusement park in Youngstown, Ohio. Loved by generations of Ohioans, it was the first carousel added to the National Register of Historic Places. When fire destroyed the park in 1984, the damaged ride was put up at auction. Once-magnificent horses and chariots, scorched and in sad shape, were nearly sold off one-by-one when artist Jane Walentas and husband David – a developer of Dumbo and Brooklyn Bridge Park – came to its rescue, bought the entire merry-go-round, and had it shipped to Brooklyn.

For more than two decades Jane restored every part to recapture its original splendor. In 2006, it was reassembled for the first time since leaving Ohio. For four more years, until completion of its outdoor site, the carousel sat idle in the window of a local warehouse, giving passers-by a preview of the park's coming attraction. In 2011, Jane's labor of love was moved to its present location and opened to the public. In 2012 it survived yet another disaster, Hurricane Sandy, damaging – fortunately – only its electronics.

Seeming to float on the river with panoramic views of the Brooklyn Bridge and Manhattan's skyline, this magical musical ride is, at heart, a tried-and-true transplanted New Yorker.

Address Brooklyn Bridge Park (at Dock Street), Brooklyn, New York 11201, Phone +1 718.222.2502, www.janescarousel.com | **Transit** Subway: York St (F); High St (A, C), Bus: B 25, B 67, B 69 | **Hours** Summer hours: Wed – Mon 11am – 7pm, closed Tue; Winter hours: Thu – Sun 11am – 6pm, closed Mon – Wed | **Tip** Nearby, Brooklyn Ice Cream Factory in a historic firehouse has all-natural ice cream treats. Walk it off with a 1.1-mile hike back to Manhattan on the scenic Brooklyn Bridge pedestrian walkway.

62___Jefferson Market Library
A castle with a clock tower

A building in the heart of the Village resembles a fairytale castle with leaded-glass windows, sloping roofs and gables, and a fire-watchtower surmounted by a clock. Built in 1877 as a courthouse, this unique edifice was deemed one of America's most beautiful structures of its day. Its courtrooms witnessed tabloid-worthy proceedings, like Harry Thaw's trial for the crime-of-passion murder of architect Stanford White (immortalized in the novel *Ragtime*); and screen siren Mae West's obscenity trial.

By 1927 the court handled only women's cases, and in 1945 it closed. Empty and abandoned for decades, it was set to be demolished when the community – including poet e.e. cummings, a Village resident – fought to preserve, restore, and repurpose this architectural treasure, and prevailed. It was transformed into a public library in 1967. The old civil court is now the adult reading room, the children's library was a police court. The brick-arched basement, once a holding area for prisoners awaiting trial, is now a reference room, home to an archive of material about the building, NYC, and in particular, Greenwich Village.

There's more to the story than the courthouse: a jail and public market were originally adjacent to it. Torn down in 1929, the jail was replaced by a Women's House of Detention. In the turbulent 1960s, among the convicted females were hardcore criminals, Vietnam War protesters, and famed political activist Angela Davis. A raucous group, inmates could be heard taunting and shouting to passersby out on the streets. Equally vociferous neighbors complained about the noise until the prison was demolished in 1973. In its place, a peaceful community garden now flourishes.

Fun to explore anytime you visit, during Open House NY (an October weekend giving access to many city venues) you can even climb the 100-foot tower's spiral stairs for a birds-eye view of historic Greenwich Village!

Address 425 Sixth Avenue (at West 10th Street), New York 10011, Phone +1 212.243.4334, www.nypl.org | Transit Subway: W 4 St (A, B, C, D, E, F, M); Christopher St-Sheridan Sq (1); 14 St (1, 2, 3, F, M, L); 8 St-NYU (N, R), Bus: M 1, M 2, M 3, M 5, M 7, M 8, M 14, M 20 | Hours Mon, Wed 10am – 8pm, Tue, Thu 11am – 6pm, Fri, Sat 10am – 5pm | Tip A brownstone with a dark past, nicknamed House of Death (14 West 10th Street), is said to be haunted by 22 ghosts, including Mark Twain, who lived there.

63 __ Katharine Hepburn Garden

Tribute to a passionate gardener

There's an enchanting garden hidden in plain sight that pays tribute to legendary film star Katharine Hepburn at the often hectic intersection of First Avenue and East 47th Street.

Open its small iron gate and wander along a path that winds through dogwood, dawn redwood, and birch trees, witch hazel, hydrangea, rhododendron, mountain laurel, and ferns. You're in a marvelous slice of woodland forest – a feast for weary urban eyes and an antidote to city stress. The path is a series of flat granite paving stones, some engraved with a witty and challenging quotation attributed to Hepburn, such as "If you always do what interests you, at least one person is pleased," and "If you survive long enough, you're revered, rather like an old building."

You'll hear songbirds, encounter stone figures of a turtle and deer, and be tempted to linger awhile to daydream on a comfortable wooden bench. Everything's designed to transport you to a place of beauty and calm. Even the bronze plaques on the south wall – with scenes from her most famous films – are subtly photo-etched so their images loom in and out of focus depending on where you stand.

It's well known that Hepburn was one of a kind – an independent, strong-minded woman who stubbornly refused to conform to stereotypes or rigid social conventions. She moved from her Connecticut family home to Manhattan's Turtle Bay neighborhood in 1932 (while performing on Broadway) and remained there until her death sixty years later. On the occasion of her ninetieth birthday in 1997, she smiled as The City of New York and the residents of Turtle Bay dedicated this miniature Eden in her name.

Neighbors knew Katharine Hepburn as a fascinating person who just happened to be a movie star. To them, she was a vocal community activist and advocate for the preservation and beautification of their charming residential enclave – and a lifelong joyous gardener.

Address Dag Hammarskjold Plaza, East 47th Street (between First and Second Avenue), New York 10017 | **Transit** Subway: Grand Central-42 St (4, 5, 6, 7, S), Bus: M 15, M 42, M 50, M 101, M 102, M 103 | **Hours** Open 24/7, daylight hours recommended | **Tip** Have a look at Hepburn's brownstone at 244 East 49th Street. The intersection at Second Avenue is named Katharine Hepburn Place.

"Sometimes I wonder if men and women really suit each other. Perhaps they should live next door and just visit now and then."

Katharine Hepburn

64__Keith Haring Mural
Whimsical swims

Dolphins fly through hoops as mermen, kids, and fantasy fish dive and romp across an 18-foot-high, 170-foot-wide concrete wall at the Carmine Street free outdoor public swimming pool. An exuberant celebration of aquatic fun rendered in bright blue, yellow, white, and black, this joyous giant mural is unmistakably the work of internationally acclaimed NY artist and social activist Keith Haring. He painted it in 1987 without a preliminary sketch, letting the inspiration of the moment and his love for city kids guide his hand. Tucked between tree-lined West Village streets, it brings smiles to local children spending sweet summer hours at the pool and dazzles anyone passing by.

Born in 1958 in Pennsylvania, Haring studied art and admired cartoonists like Walt Disney. He moved to NYC in the early eighties to continue his art education, then joined a downtown scene of young graffiti artists and punk, hip hop, and dance musicians shaking up the established art world. City dwellers first spotted his distinctive outline figures drawn on blank ad spaces in the subways. Gallery shows and public works attracted a far wider audience to his bold-lined renditions of birth, life, love, death, sex, and war. Openly gay, unafraid to portray erotic imagery, and intent on raising public consciousness, his art often espoused a social message. In 1986, he founded Pop Shop – a store based on the esthetic that *art is for everybody* – selling inexpensive objects (key chains, pins, tee shirts) featuring his images, with all shop proceeds donated to programs that support art in city schools, oppose apartheid, and fund research to conquer AIDS.

Tragically, Keith Haring was only thirty-one when he succumbed to AIDS in 1990. His art lives on in exhibitions and museum collections, enjoyed every day by ordinary folks around the world in hospitals, day care centers, playgrounds. And at this cool summertime pool.

Address 1 Clarkson Street (near Seventh Avenue), New York 10014, Phone +1 212.242.5228 | **Transit** Subway: Houston St (1); W 4 St (A, B, C, D, E, F, M), Bus: M 5, M 20, M 21 | **Hours** Jul. 4 – Labor Day (early Sep.) daily 11am – 3pm and 4 – 7pm | **Tip** The picturesque front stoop from TVs *Cosby Show* isn't in Brooklyn; it's actually at 10 Saint Luke's Place, on the north side of the pool.

65__Library Way

Words of wisdom underfoot

When you walk the city's streets, it makes sense to glance down at the sidewalk to prevent a random mishap. You may trip on uneven pavement, or ruin your fancy shoes in a muddy puddle. In residential areas you pay attention to the street lest you step in dog poo.

One place where you'll really enjoy examining what's underfoot is Library Way, the two-block stretch of East 41st Street spanning Park, Madison, and Fifth Avenues. Embedded in the sidewalk are 96 sculpted bronze plaques, each inscribed with a thought-provoking quotation from a literary giant, artist, scientist, or philosopher – with images inspired by the text.

This idea was co-developed by the Grand Central Partnership and New York Public Library to enhance the sidewalks leading to the library's iconic main-branch building. An impressive committee comprised of authors, scholars, librarians, and editors of *The New Yorker* selected quotes to best reflect the impact of creative minds on society. A Greenwich Village artist, Gregg LeFevre, was commissioned to design and execute the plaques.

It's almost impossible to view them on a weekday without impeding the constant flow of pedestrians crowding these midtown streets. To best appreciate the entire scope of Library Way, the beauty of its words and evocative art, visit on a Sunday when foot traffic is sparse. Begin your walk at Park Avenue and 41st Street and head west toward the library. The wise words of 45 brilliant thinkers (11 women, 34 men) come to life in the pavement. You'll discover a wealth of *bon mots* beneath your feet: "Truth exists, only falsehood has to be invented." (Georges Braque); "Books are the treasured wealth of the world and the fit inheritance of generations and nations." (Henry David Thoreau); "Remarks are not literature." (Gertrude Stein).

Keep your eyes on the ground, your head in the clouds. Look down at each – and find your favorite.

Address East 41st Street (between Park and Fifth Avenue), New York 10017 |
Transit Subway: 42 St-Bryant Park (B, D, F, M); 5 Av (7); Grand Central-42 St (S, 4, 5, 6, 7), Bus: M 1, M 2, M 3, M 4, M 5, M 7, M 42, M 101, M 102, M 103 | Tip Browse 3 floors of international books, periodicals, and a huge Japanese anime and manga section at Kinokuniya (1073 Avenue of the Americas).

Where the press is free, and every man able to read, all is safe.

— Thomas Jefferson (1743-1826), "Letter to Colonel Charles Yancey"

66_ The Louis Armstrong House

Satchmo's home sweet home

Internationally acclaimed and beloved jazz trumpeter, composer, and singer Louis Armstrong, whose wide smile earned him the nickname Satchmo (short for satchel mouth), could have lived in a mansion, but from 1943 until his death in 1971, he came home to a modest brick house in Corona, Queens, on a street where ordinary working-class folks lived. It's still a leafy, family-friendly neighborhood, and the house is now a National Historic Landmark where you can glimpse the private life of an icon.

Louis met his fourth wife, Lucille, when she was the only dark-complexioned dancer at the Cotton Club (which required performers to have skin "lighter than a brown paper bag"). They wed in 1942. Since he toured ten months out of the year, Lucille felt he needed a place to call home between gigs, to relax and enjoy his favorite meal of red beans and rice. While he was on the road, she secretly bought this cozy house.

There's much to see and hear on the escorted tour. Mementos and gifts from royalty and international heads of state are in the living room, and although the marble- and mirrored-wall bathroom appeared in *Time* magazine, and the blue-enameled kitchen's a gem, Pops' most treasured space was his upstairs den. There he'd chat with pals, in person or by phone, correspond with fans, and document his legacy on reel-to-reel tapes of both music and numerous personal conversations – bits of which you'll get to hear in each room! Standing on the balcony he'd play his trumpet to let the neighbors know he was home, and they'd come out in the street to welcome him back.

A vast archive of his personal papers, photos, and recordings stored a few miles away at Queens College will move in 2017 to a visitor's center being built opposite the house.

Enjoy year-round events like jazz afternoons and soirees in the garden, talks, educational programs – and a gift shop that rocks!

Address 34–56 107th Street (near 37th Avenue), Corona, New York 11368, Phone +1 718.478.8274, www.louisarmstronghouse.org, info@louisarmstronghouse.org | **Transit** Subway: 103 St-Corona Plaza (7), Bus: Q19, Q23, Q48, Q66 | **Hours** Tue – Fri 10am – 5pm, Sat – Sun noon – 5pm | **Tip** Visit Lemon Ice King of Corona to taste Italian ices in mouthwatering flavors that have been neighborhood favorites for more than seventy years.

67 __ Mahayana Buddha
Meditation amidst chaos

You'll find the biggest Buddha in all of New York City seated majestically inside what was formerly an adult movie theater at the foot of the Manhattan Bridge.

Mahayana Buddhist Temple, the oldest Chinese Buddhist temple on the East Coast, was founded on Mott Street in 1962 by Annie Ying, funded by profits from her husband's chain of gift shops. Initially created as a community center for displaced Chinese men who had come to America to earn money then return to their families at home, Mahayana became the city's largest Buddhist temple when it relocated to Canal Street in 1996.

Two fierce golden lions guard its bright red doors, warding off evil spirits. All others are welcome. Beyond the entrance is a simply decorated room. A display case contains treasures and trinkets for sale – teapots, beaded bracelets, mini-Buddhas and such. A small Buddha sits at the center of this anteroom to the temple. Further inside is a statue of Guan Yin, Goddess of Mercy and Compassion. A dollar donation entitles you to extract a tiny scroll from a bowl of rolled-up fortunes. A dollar more buys a stick of incense. When you've read your fortune and said a quiet prayer, follow a hallway leading to the main chamber – and an awe-inspiring sight. At the front of what appears to be a huge, ornately decorated banquet hall sits a 16-foot-tall golden Buddha backlit by a neon-blue halo.

Seated upon a giant lotus, he seems to pulsate with color and light. Despite your surroundings – the lavish decor, scent of incense, offerings of fruit and flowers – this glowing Buddha is what captures your full attention. Here, on one of the busiest, most heavily trafficked streets in Chinatown, you can find relaxation, peace, and serenity. Whether you stay to meditate or walk around to view the drawings depicting events in the life of the Buddha, you'll savor your singular experience beneath his radiant, benevolent gaze.

Address 133 Canal Street (between Bowery and Chrystie Street), New York 10002, Phone +1 212.925.8787, http://en.mahayana.us, mahayana@mahayana.us |
Transit Subway: Grand St (B, D); Canal St (J, N, Q, R, Z, 6); East Broadway (F), Bus: M 9, M 15, M 22, M 103 | **Hours** Daily 8:30am – 6pm | **Tip** Dazzling displays of diamonds, jade, and 24-karat gold illuminate the windows of Chinatown's jewelry district along the intersection of Bowery & Canal Street.

68 Manhattan Night Court

A nice place to visit but …

Two popular American TV shows, *Night Court* and *Law and Order*, were inspired by the real-life drama that's played out every night in downtown Manhattan. Curious visitors – locals on a cheap date, students, journalists, tourists – might well expect to be entertained. On a good night, proceedings may turn out to be hilarious or melodramatic. And sometimes a big-name celebrity gets hauled in by the cops.

New York State law requires that anyone who is arrested must be promptly brought before a judge to determine if there's sufficient cause to charge them with an offense. This first step in the criminal justice process is the arraignment, and it takes place at the Manhattan Criminal Courts Building every day of the year. It's always open to the public. Night Court (arraignments held between 5pm and 1am) began in 1907, when it became apparent that day sessions alone couldn't accommodate all the arrests.

There's no way to know what you'll find inside the courtroom. Every night nearly a hundred cases are heard, on offenses ranging from stealing a six-pack of beer to murder. The front row is reserved for defendants. Some have private attorneys but most are represented by court-appointed public defenders. The accused and the defense lawyer stand before the judge while a prosecutor, an Assistant District Attorney representing the State, reads the charges. A plea is entered (guilty, not guilty, or no contest). The judge rules. For minor offenses, the defendant is usually fined and released. In the case of serious crimes, the judge decides whether to grant bail or hold the individual in custody pending trial.

There's a metal detector at the courthouse entrance and a security guard will inspect your bag. Tell the officer you want to observe Night Court and you'll be directed to two active courtrooms. Find the liveliest, walk in, take a seat. And be glad you're free to walk out whenever you want.

CRIMINAL COURTS BUILDING

Address 100 Centre Street (between Hogan Place and White Street), New York 10013 | **Transit** Subway: Brooklyn Bridge-City Hall (4, 5, 6); Canal St (J, N, Q, R, 6), Bus: M5, M9, M15, M22, M103 | **Hours** Daily 5pm–1am (including weekends and holidays) | **Tip** Gobble up outrageously delicious crab soup dumplings – the soup is inside the dumplings – at Joe's Shanghai (9 Pell Street).

69 Marjorie Eliot's Sunday Salon

Love, and all that jazz

She greets you at the door with a smile that feels like a hug. With a halo of curls and clad in a flowing caftan, she's the wonderful cool Auntie you wish you'd had. Every Sunday afternoon, Miss Marjorie Eliot welcomes perfect strangers to drop by her apartment for two hours of incomparable live jazz. This weekly ritual began in 1992 as a tribute to her late son Phillip – and it's free! Fifty or so folding chairs arranged in the foyer, kitchen, and living room are made comfier with puffy seat cushions. Lace curtains filter sunlight into the room, a delicate floral scent (maybe her cologne?) fills the air, and even if you don't know a soul there, you feel you're relaxing among family and friends.

It's a thrill when the music begins, hard to describe in mere words. Marjorie and son Rudel Drears take turns at the upright piano (he sings too), and with a changing cast of players on trumpet, flute, sax, clarinet, and bass, they make musical magic. Old-time jazz greats and rising young stars appear, often together for the first time, playing new riffs on familiar tunes as well as fresh improvisation. The musicians adore these private jams, performing for such an intimate audience. Love and gratitude are expressed with thunderous applause, especially for gracious host Miss Marjorie. While the juice and granola bar snack she passes around make you smile, passing Sunday afternoon here feeds your soul.

All this goes down in an uptown landmark Beaux Arts building whose street corner signs read *W 160 Street/Count Basie Place/ Edgecombe Avenue/Paul Robeson Boulevard*. Basie, singer-actor Robeson, chanteuse Lena Horne, and boxer Joe Louis once lived at this architectural gem in Sugar Hill – a legendary enclave that Harlem's black elite have called home since the 1940s.

Your first visit will be unforgettable. Whether you're coming from Bombay or Brooklyn you'll be back another Sunday.

Address 555 Edgecombe Avenue (at West 160th Street), Studio 3F, New York 10032, Phone +1 212.781.6595 | Transit Subway: 163 St-Amsterdam Av (C), Bus: M2, M3, M4, M5, M100, M101 | Hours Sun 3:30–5:30pm | Tip 409 Edgecombe Avenue was home to W.E.B. DuBois, a towering figure in the fight for social justice and Thurgood Marshall, first African-American Supreme Court Justice.

70__Math Playground
Discovery is way cool

A whole lot more fun than you or your kids might ever imagine, MoMath, as it's popularly known, shines a colorful spotlight on the creative, exploratory, and engaging aspects of mathematics. The only mathematics museum in North America, it's dedicated to invigorating math's dull-as-a-doorknob reputation.

Museum founder Greg Whitney says, "People love something to touch." So from its π-shaped front door handles to an exciting and varied assortment of hands-on constructions, projections, light- and sound-effects, worktables, floor puzzles, and mechanical exhibits spread out over 20,000 square feet covering two floors, the entire exhibition space is designed to spark curiosity and delight. Though the 31 math-themed stations are primarily geared to kids aged seven to twelve, there's more than enough technology for toddlers, teens, and adults to enjoy as well.

Touch-screens provide instructions for most of the interactive installations. Friendly young guides are on hand to explain the lessons of the displays and will enthusiastically engage in conversation concerning math and the museum. Kids can pedal one of two square-wheeled tricycles over a bright yellow, bumpy circular track, or stretch agile legs across the Math Square, an animated, neon-lit game that looks like a disco floor a la *Saturday Night Fever*. Exhibit names are seriously intriguing – Coaster Rollers, Formula Morph, Polypaint, Light Grooves, Logo Generator, Human Tree, and Shapes of Space to name just a few. For keepsakes, the in-house gift shop offers a well-curated array of fascinating items, including challenging games and puzzles, posters, as well as MoMath souvenir merchandise. For ecology-minded reasons, those seeking a brochure are directed to the MoMath website.

According to co-director Cindy Lawrence, the guiding principle of the museum is that "math *IS* cool and we're going to show you it's cool."

Address The Museum of Mathematics (MoMath), 11 East 26th Street (between Madison and Fifth Avenue), New York 10010, Phone +1 212.542.0566, www.momath.org, info@momath.org | Transit Subway: 28 St (6, N, R), Bus: M1, M2, M3, M5, M102, M103 | Hours Daily 10am – 5pm | Tip Madison Square Park, right across the street, hosts seasonal sculpture installations. Find great burgers, fries, and shakes at the city's original Shake Shack location, inside the park, near Madison Avenue & 23rd Street.

71__Merchant's House
The Tredwells at home

Open the column-flanked front door of this stately East 4th Street townhouse and you're swept into the nineteenth century, entering the elegant home of Seabury Tredwell. It seems he's out for an afternoon stroll with his wife and eight children. While you wait for them to return, have a look around.

Inside the formal double parlor featuring matching bronze etched-glass chandeliers and magnificent black-and-gold marble mantels, you'll see fine furniture, a rare piano, paintings, elaborately framed mirrors, crystal candlesticks and decanters. Look up at the ceiling's roundels and moldings, exceptional examples of ornamental plasterwork.

Downstairs is the family parlor and a well-equipped kitchen (with ovens, stove, pie safe, sink, and worktable) whose door opens onto a garden. Upstairs, an alcove study adjoins well-appointed bedrooms, each with regal canopy beds draped in damask and rich velvet. At the top of the stairs is a storeroom and servants' quarters.

Wealthy hardware merchant Seabury Tredwell bought the house in 1835, when this was Manhattan's most fashionable neighborhood. His family lived there for nearly a century. Daughter Gertrude, born 1840, was the last Tredwell to occupy the house. From the 1870s until her death in 1933, she preserved its original state with only two updates: electricity and indoor plumbing. She rarely ventured outdoors; over the years, the once-stylish enclave had become populated by flophouses and unsavory characters. After her death, a cousin rescued the house from the wrecking ball, made needed repairs, and opened it as a museum.

In recent years, the area has made a comeback. Amid chic boutiques and pricey cafes, Merchant's House remains exquisitely unchanged. Come for a tour and return for new exhibits, performances, concerts, and the spooky Halloween event – when it's rumored that a few of the Tredwell kids come out to play.

Address 29 East 4th Street (between Bowery and Lafayette Street), New York 10003, Phone +1 212.777.1089, www.merchantshouse.org, info@merchantshouse.org | **Transit** Subway: 8 St-NYU (N, R); Bleecker St (6); Broadway-Lafayette St (B, D, F, M), Bus: M 1, M 2, M 3, M 5, M 8, M 15, M 101, M 102, M 103 | **Hours** Thu–Mon noon–5pm | **Tip** The anti-slavery speech delivered by Abraham Lincoln at Cooper Union (on Astor Place) in 1860 was so compelling it attracted national attention and led to his nomination for the presidency.

72__ The Microcosm
A roomful of ordinary oddities

What do a man's shoe, phony international ID cards, dozens of plastic spoons, a bag of gummy-worms, and a videotape of sixties porn king Al Goldstein (*Screw* mag) have in common? Give up? These are only a handful of the quirky and evocative modern-age relics arranged with great care on shelves lining the walls of a defunct Tribeca freight elevator. Welcome to Mmuseumm, a tiny urban cubicle that bills itself as the world's smallest natural history museum.

Its curators gather found objects from all over – many of them donated by global 'collectors' – to engage museumgoers in an experience that's an "exploration of the proof of our existence." Every little item on display is believed capable of telling an exponentially larger story about contemporary life.

The shoe is the very one hurled by a protestor at President George W. Bush in Baghdad, 2008. This missile of political dissent shares shelf space with the crushed remains of two hundred New Delhi mosquitoes caught mid-bite by one man over three months. Nearby is a display of NYC artist Maira Kalman's collection of tufts of moss. Many artifacts are beyond bizarre exactly *because of their ordinariness*. And where else would you encounter – in the same gallery – Down's Syndrome dolls, peep-show coins, souvenir Saddam Hussein wristwatches, counterfeit Sharpie markers, toothpaste tubes from around the world, and inflatable pool toys censored by the Saudi Arabian government?

The collection changes every six months. On weekends between early spring and late fall, you can view individual exhibits comprising disparate global ephemera. No more than three visitors at once fit inside the museum, and sharing your impressions with the others only adds to the fun. The curators encourage public submissions, so feel free to propose an exhibition of your prized vintage airline soap, matchbooks, or bakery string. You may be the next artist on display.

Address 4 Cortlandt Alley (between Franklin and White Street), New York 10013, www.Mmuseumm.com, info@Mmuseumm.com | Transit Subway: Franklin St (1, 2); Canal St (A, C, E, J, N, Q, R, Z, 6); City Hall (4, 5, 6), Bus: M5, M9, M20, M22, M103 | Hours Early spring to late fall (check website) Sat–Sun noon–6pm | Tip Have weekend brunch at Bubby's (120 Hudson Street), famous for its house-cured bacon and seasonal choices of homemade pies.

73__Modern Pinball
Flipping out in the city

Pinball is back! Bells ring, lights flash and steel balls roll! Lining the walls of this playland is a super-duper collection of new and restored pinball machines that the owners call "amusement park rides under glass." Wall Street types, hipsters, baby boomers, kids on stepstools, even players who fancy themselves the best in the world tackle more than 30 of the greatest pinball games ever created. Standouts include StarTrek, KISS, Addams Family, Simpsons, Metallica, and Punchy the Clown.

Every game's a unique experience, never the same twice. It's interactive and hands-on, flooded with sounds, dazzling lights, wildly intricate mechanics, and explosive technicolor art. The game was once considered a corrupter of youth, a form of gambling that robbed kids of their lunch money, and in 1942 Mayor Fiorello LaGuardia banned it. In 1976 advocates proved pinball was a game of skill, not luck – and the ban was lifted.

World headquarters of the International Flipper Pinball Association (IFPA), Modern Pinball NYC serves up pinball with a new twist: no coins required. Pay for a unit of time, by the hour or an all-day pass, then play to your heart's content. Get strategy tips from staff or even arrange a lesson with a pro.

Love a machine? You can buy it! Prices go from $5,000 to a small fortune, and every dollar spent playing is applied toward a future purchase. No alcohol or food is sold on site, but a wristband lets you come and go freely – and a nearby pub will take ten percent off your check.

Founder and tournament champ Steve Zahler – ranked #1 in New York, #34 worldwide in 2014 – got hooked on pinball when he was five and it's been his passion ever since. He and co-founder Steve Epstein are warriors for pinball's future as both family-friendly pastime and competitive sport. A cool destination for dates, special events, and birthday parties, Modern Pinball NYC is flippin' good fun.

Address 362 Third Avenue (between East 26th and 27th Street), New York 10016, Phone +1 646.415.8440, www.modernpinballnyc.com, info@modernpinballnyc.com | **Transit** Subway: 28 St (6, R, N), Bus: M 1, M 3, M 9, M 15, M 23, M 34, M 101, M 102, M 103 | **Hours** Sun – Wed 11am – midnight, Thu – Sat 11am – 2am | **Tip** Feast your senses at Little India's aromatic spice shops and restaurants along Lexington Avenue from 26th to 30th Streets.

74 Morbid Anatomy
The dark mysteries of life

Not the cobwebby attic you might expect when you hear its name, the Morbid Anatomy Museum is located in a recently renovated, well-lit, and spacious three-floor space. Its street-level entrance opens to an inviting cafe and shop whose shelves and display cases offer a playful and weird assortment of books on subjects like medical oddities, taxidermy, funeral arts, and death imagery. Sip a latte while you leaf through the museum's own recently published, fascinating book, *The Morbid Anatomy Anthology*.

Climb upstairs to explore two remarkable galleries. The first displays temporary exhibits (on loan from private collections) of objects beautiful and bizarre that pose provocative questions and evoke complex emotions about "the places where death and beauty intersect."

A second gallery contains a one-of-a-kind research library (more than 2,000 e-books) and the museum's permanent collection of medical specimens, taxidermy, skeletal parts, anatomical art, death masks, human-hair mourning jewelry, and other eerie difficult-to-categorize stuff.

This collection once was stored in the closet of its founder and creative director Joanna Ebenstein, a bright-eyed, upbeat book designer and photographer whose enthusiasm for morbid imagery began at an early age and intensified over time. She explored fine art depictions of death in medical and art museums around the world, amassed books and artifacts, lectured, and wrote a popular blog on the subject. Thanks to private investors, Kickstarter internet funding, and a hardworking board of directors, Morbid Anatomy Museum – the collection's new home – opened its doors in 2014.

Special events are held downstairs, below the cafe. Creative and whimsical taxidermy and craft workshops; lectures by scholars, morticians, spiritualists, and artists; and death-themed film screenings contextualize the collections, shining light on shadowy mysteries.

Address 424-A 3rd Avenue (at 7th Street), Brooklyn, New York 11215, Phone +1 347.799.1017, www.morbidanatomymuseum.org, info@morbidanatomymuseum.org | Transit Subway: 4 Av (F, G); 9 St (R), Bus: B 37, B 61, B 63, B 103 | Hours Mon and Wed–Sun noon–6pm, closed Tue | Tip Four & Twenty Blackbirds on 3rd Avenue & 8th Street bakes a salted caramel apple pie that makes you glad to be alive.

75 Morris-Jumel Mansion

George Washington slept here

A few steps past a busy food market on St. Nicholas Avenue lies a path to another time and place. The urban landscape vanishes as you stroll Sylvan Terrace, a cobblestone lane of matching wood-frame row houses. At its end stands a genteel Georgian-style mansion that evokes colonial Virginia.

Atop Manhattan's highest point, in a cozy park of historic trees and English gardens, is a white-painted house with tall graceful columns that flank the entrance door and support a triangular pediment. Its elegant rooms are furnished with period decor reflecting various chapters in its history. Explore the first-floor parlor, dining room, sitting room, and rare (the first of its kind in the US) octagonal drawing room. Peek into second-floor bedrooms and contemplate its illustrious occupants.

Morris-Jumel is Manhattan's oldest surviving residence, built in 1765 as a summer villa for British Colonel Roger Morris and his wife. The British-loyalist Morrises fled as the American Revolution began. George Washington made it his headquarters, directing the Battle of Harlem Heights from its lofty perch. A decade later it was repurposed as an elegant inn where newly elected President Washington attended a formal dinner. Wealthy French shipping magnate Stephen Jumel bought the stately mansion in 1810. When he died, his wife Eliza inherited a massive fortune and married former Vice President Aaron Burr. Three years after Burr moved in, Eliza filed for divorce and lived there until her death.

Don't miss standout pieces original to the house. Aaron Burr's 'metamorphic desk' transforms from a combination desk-and-chair to an oval table; and Eliza's bed purportedly once belonged to Empress Josephine. Washington slept here in the eighteenth century, but today it's far from a sleepy place. Provocative cultural and educational programs, festivals, neighborhood tours, and jazz concerts excite your imagination.

Address 65 Jumel Terrace (between West 160th and 162nd Street), New York 10032, Phone +1 212.923.8008, www.morrisjumel.org, info@morrisjumel.org | Transit Subway: 163 St-Amsterdam Av (C), Bus: M2, M3, M4, M5, M100, M101 | Hours Tue–Sun 10am–4pm | Tip Walk to St Nicholas Park to explore Hamilton Grange. American Revolutionary patriot Alexander Hamilton lived in this house until his death in a historic 1804 duel with political enemy Aaron Burr.

76__ The Mossman Collection
Lure of the lock

Finding the John M. Mossman Lock Collection is half the fun. It's demurely tucked away on the second-floor balcony of a building that has housed the General Society of Mechanics & Tradesmen of the City of New York since 1899. The philanthropic Society, founded in 1785 to promote educational and cultural programs, is home to the Mechanics Institute, the city's oldest privately-endowed, tuition-free, technical school for working tradesfolk. This blue-collar outpost sits proudly on the same block as its pedigree neighbors: the Harvard Club, NYC Bar Association, and New York Yacht Club.

Tell the security guard you'd like to see the Lock Collection, sign a visitor log, pay a modest fee, and receive a loaner copy of *The Lure of the Lock*. Mossman's 1928 book (available for sale if you wish to keep it) describes in detail each of nearly four hundred items on display, and even recounts tales of famous bank heists.

You'll be escorted up a marble staircase to a balcony area perched above the Society's huge, elegant library (incidentally, the city's second-oldest) covered by an enormous skylight. Then you're on your own to peer inside old-fashioned display cases containing the world's most comprehensive collection of antique locking mechanisms from banks, vaults, and other sources, with some examples dating back as far as 4000 BC.

The range of materials, shapes, and sizes is impressive. Many pieces bear exquisite hand-tooled ornamentation and elaborate artistic designs. Some are partially disassembled so you can view their innards and marvel at the ingenuity and workmanship developed over the centuries to protect cash and valuables.

A uniquely fascinating treasure trove for the general public, it's a must-see attraction for visiting locksmiths and, well, yes — lock-pickers. To discourage those who might find it hard to resist temptation, many of the display cases are securely triple-locked!

Address 20 West 44th Street (between Fifth Avenue and Avenue of the Americas), New York 10036, Phone +1 212.840.1840, www.generalsociety.org/ | **Transit** Subway: 42 St-Bryant Pk (B, D, F, M); Grand Central-42 St (4, 5, 6, 7, S); Times Sq-42 St (1, 2, 3, 7, N, Q, R); 5 Av (7); Bus: M1, M2, M3, M4, M5, M7, M20, M42, M50, M101, M102, M103, M104 | **Hours** Mon–Thu 11am–7pm, Fri 10am–5pm (call to verify) | **Tip** At 110 West 44th Street view the National Debt Clock, displaying the current US gross national debt and each American family's portion of that debt.

77 __Mount Vernon Hotel & Garden

A country escape, inside the city

In the shadow of the 59th Street Bridge, wedged between high-rise buildings, is a stone carriage house built in 1799 on what was then a 23-acre estate owned by Abigail Adams Smith (daughter of American president John Adams) and her husband. In 1826, the building was sold and converted into the Mount Vernon Hotel, a country getaway for New Yorkers and visitors from abroad. It was advertised as "free from the noise and dust of the public roads, and fitted up and intended for only the most genteel and respectable" clientele. The northern end of New York City was then only at 14th Street. A stagecoach or steamboat excursion up to the hotel led to a day of East River swimming, strolls though gardens and wooded paths, turtle soup and oyster suppers, and sunny afternoons playing cards in the gentlemen's tavern, or exchanging recipes, gossip, and pleasantries in the ladies' parlor.

After a series of owners over the next century, the hotel was purchased in 1924 by a preservation organization, The Colonial Dames of America, which opened it to the public in 1939, and has meticulously cared for it ever since.

Step through the front door midday from Tuesday through Sunday and you'll be warmly greeted by a docent to escort you on a personalized tour of the house – with its unique collection of decorative arts and print materials – and its grounds. The tour, starting with a brief film featuring the property's fascinating history, is geared to suit your particular interests.

Outside, have a close look at the stone facade and notice its date of origin embedded in the pattern. A stroll in the garden is heavenly. Linger amid the trees, plantings, stone paths, the romantic gazebo. A bird sings. A squirrel scampers across the path. The air seems sweeter, less urban. The Mount Vernon Hotel has worked its magic – you've escaped!

Address 421 East 61st Street (between First and York Avenue), New York 10065, Phone +1 212.838.6878, www.mvhm.org | **Transit** Subway: Lexington Av-59 St (N, R, 4, 5, 6); Lexington Av-63 St (F), Bus: M 15, M 31, M 57 | **Hours** Tue – Sun 11am – 4pm | **Tip** While browsing in the gift shop, have a look at the schedule of special monthly museum events. You'll be tempted to return for a lecture, candlelit mystery hunt, or musicale.

78__Nevelson's Chapel of Tranquility

White Light

A dazzling white-on-white space designed for contemplation, the Chapel of the Good Shepherd at St. Peter's Lutheran Church is American artist Louise Nevelson's only permanent sculptural environment in New York City. This small five-sided chapel, in which Nevelson sought to create a "place of purity," was consecrated in 1977. Commissioned by its reverend and congregation, it was donated by parishioner Erol Beker, a Turkish-born industrialist, whose remains are inurned within the chapel.

Nevelson's genius is expressed in a breathtaking white-painted assemblage of found wooden objects arranged on the chapel's five white walls. The pews and altar are of bleached ash, and the window is frosted white. The only non-white surface is the gold-leafed Cross of the Good Shepherd behind the altar.

The visitor is struck by the utter tranquility here. Contemporary and spare in its simplicity, this is a sacred place. It is interesting to note that though she herself was Jewish, Louise Nevelson created a Christian liturgical space that many say evokes a spiritual experience to rival that of grand cathedrals.

Exit the chapel to explore St. Peter's skylight-lit interior and the beauty of its Sanctuary and works of art, including Arnaldo Pomodoro's dramatic exterior cross, a sixteenth-century Dutch cross, a weaving by Ann Sherwin Bromberg, and processional crosses by William Cordaroy and Kiki Smith.

St. Peter's commitment to the creative and performing arts is an essential expression of its mission. Known as the jazz church, it celebrates jazz as a spiritual force for the community. Sunday nights at 5pm St. Peter's conducts Jazz Vespers, a worship service where local musicians and visitors from around the world come to play – and where all are welcome to pray and reflect.

Address 619 Lexington Avenue (between East 53rd and 54th Street), New York 10022, Phone +1 212.935.2200, www.saintpeters.org | Transit Subway: Lexington Av-53 St (E, M); 51 St (6), Bus: M 31, M 50, M 57, M 101, M 102, M 103 | Hours Daily 8:30am – 8pm | Tip St. Peter's hosts year-round jazz, classical, and choral concerts and an acclaimed annual Bach Festival. It is also home to the off-Broadway York Theater Company. Check the website for performance information.

79__The News Building
Superman worked here

Walk through its imposing Art Deco entrance and you've landed in the lobby of the *Daily Planet*, the setting of the fictional newspaper where Clark Kent and Lois Lane worked as reporters!

Built in 1930 as headquarters of the actual *New York Daily News* – the city's first tabloid, boasting the biggest newspaper circulation anywhere – it was New York's first flat-top skyscraper, which Ayn Rand smugly labeled "the ugliest building in the city." Publisher-owner Joseph Patterson hired famed architect Raymond Hood (who later designed Rockefeller Center) to create a building not only to house the paper's printing plant and offices, but to proclaim its position at the center of the world. Expressing this is the lobby's centerpiece – the world's largest indoor globe, a 12-foot-diameter glowing orb, slowly rotating inside a recessed, circular mirrored pit. On the floor around it, compass points and brass markers measure distances between NYC – the epicenter – and other cities of the world. A black glass-domed ceiling suggests far reaches of the universe. Conceived as an educational exhibit, the lobby is a notable architectural site and still fascinates visitors, with its world clocks, vintage dials, and gizmos along the walls.

The *Daily News* saw itself as having a global perspective, with its finger on the pulse of the common man. Sculptor Rene Chambellan created the striking three-story-tall bas-relief on its facade depicting the building as a radiant beacon above figures of working people. Huge carved letters proclaim HE MADE SO MANY OF THEM, a reference to Abraham Lincoln's quote: "God must have loved the common people, he made so many of them."

The edifice was renamed the News Building in 1995 when the real *Daily News* moved elsewhere. But the irresistible charm of the Deco period and the aura of the imaginary *Daily Planet* lives on.

Address 220 East 42nd Street (between Second and Third Avenue), New York 10017 | **Transit** Subway: Grand Central-42 St (4, 5, 6, 7, S), Bus: M 1, M 2, M 3, M 4, M 15, M 42, M 101, M 102, M 103 | **Hours** Mon – Fri 9am – 5pm | **Tip** Another iconic Raymond Hood flat-top is the GE Building (formerly RCA Building). TV viewers know it as *30 Rock*. Views from its observation deck, Top Of The Rock, are outstanding.

80 __Nuyorican Poets Cafe
Breaking barriers

If the idea of a poetry reading conjures up images of a bespectacled *artiste* droning on before neat rows of literati politely stifling yawns, prepare to have that notion blown away at the Nuyorican Poets Cafe.

This exhilarating performing arts shrine and East Village bar celebrates creative energy, nurturing artists of all genres, ethnicities, ages, and inclinations who are under-represented in mainstream media. They explode traditional artist/spectator boundaries and get fired up by vigorous audience participation. Join the line winding round the block before the doors open and meet a remarkable cross-section of people from around the world and across the street gathered for an action-packed evening.

The Cafe's originator – writer, poet, and college professor Miguel Algarin – fervently believed "we must listen to one another, respect one another's habits, and share the truth and integrity that the voice of the poet so generously provides." What began in 1973 with kindred spirits coming together in Algarin's living room rapidly grew, necessitating a move in 1975 to a nearby Irish tavern. In 1980, by then a nonprofit arts organization, NPC bought its permanent home on East 3rd Street.

The online events calendar describes a vast variety of poetry slams, hip hop, jazz, theater, video, visual arts, comedy, and more on what's billed as "the biggest little stage on earth." While one-time performances and hard-to-categorize events pepper the calendar, there is a weekly pattern: Mondays are open-mike nights, Wednesdays open slams, Latin jazz on Thursdays, legendary poetry slams on Fridays. Weekends see a wide-ranging array of entertainment. Tickets are reasonably priced at the door (slightly higher when purchased online), and well worth the unforgettable experience inside. Prepare yourself to become actively involved in whatever's going on that night. Polite audiences need not apply.

Address 236 East 3rd Street (between Avenues B and C), New York 10009,
Phone +1 212.780.9386, www.nuyorican.org, info@nuyorican.org | Transit Subway:
2 Av (F, V), Bus: M14A, M15 | Hours Hours change, depending on performance
schedule. Check online or call. | Tip Avenues A, B, C and adjacent numbered streets are
known to locals as Alphabet City. Allow time to explore this hip, shabby-chic district of
bistros, bars, galleries, and trendy boutiques.

81__ The NY Earth Room
The complexity of simplicity

It's a room filled with dirt. That's all. 250 cubic yards of soil, covering 3,600 square feet of floor space, 22 inches deep, weighing 280,000 pounds.

Ring the outdoor buzzer and climb a steep flight of stairs to a rather typical white-walled SoHo gallery space. It's quiet. There's usually nobody there except for a man seated solemnly behind a desk at the far end. Straight ahead is the reason you're here.

You might giggle at first, perhaps shake your head in disbelief. That's okay. But wait. Let go of your gallery-going expectations. Stop. Breathe. Close, and then reopen, your eyes. Inhale the primal loamy scent. Stay silent as it creeps inside you and speaks of what's inexpressible in words. Experience its depth, breadth, weight. Suspend judgment and let the magic in.

Sculptor Walter De Maria was a major presence in the New York art scene from the early 1960s until his death in 2013. A pioneer of Minimalism and Conceptual Art, he cultivated an ability to make the simple complex. His land-art projects, executed on a monumental scale, came to be known as Earthworks. He was a musician as well – with Lou Reed and John Cale in the *Primitives*, a band that later became the *Velvet Underground*.

De Maria maintained a low public profile in the face of national and international acclaim, questioning the value of temporary art exhibitions. One stated goal of Dia, where the work is housed, is to "bring the art to a place and let it speak over time." Dia Art Foundation – with multiple sites in and around New York City – was established to commission and support often highly idiosyncratic, permanent installations of contemporary art. Ever true to its commitment, Dia has scrupulously maintained – watered, raked, and de-molded – *The New York Earth Room* since 1980.

It's not advertised. You hear about it from someone who heard about it from someone else who heard about it. Don't miss it.

Dia Art Foundation
Walter De Maria
The New York Earth Room, 1977

press 2B
walk up to 2nd foor
open Wednesday–Sunday
12–3pm and 3:30–6pm
closed summer months
www.diaart.org

Address The New York Earth Room at Dia Art Foundation, 141 Wooster Street (near Prince Street), New York 10012, www.earthroom.org | **Transit** Subway: Prince St (N, R); Broadway-Lafayette (B, D, F, M); Spring St (A, C, E); Bleecker St (6); Houston St (1), Bus: M5, M20, M21, M103 | **Hours** Sept.–June Wed–Sun noon–6pm (closed 3–3:30pm) | **Tip** For an entirely different yet equally arresting meditation on silence and stillness – composed of brass rods – visit De Maria's *The Broken Kilometer*, steps away at 393 West Broadway.

82 — Oldest Manhole Cover
Keeping a lid on it

Could this be a portal to the Ninja Turtles' secret lair? Not quite. According to urban legend, sewers and tunnels beneath the city's elaborate manhole covers are the domain of far creepier mutant reptiles – alligators! How is this possible? New Yorkers returning from Florida vacations in the 1950s would bring home a cute baby alligator as a souvenir. When the critters grew larger, they got flushed down the toilet to sewers where (the legend claims) they ate rubbish and rats, and still prowl through the sewer system.

New York's oldest lid on this underworld is on Jersey Street, a tiny, ungentrified SoHo alley. Its time-worn surface reads CROTON AQUEDUCT 1866, marking access to an original conduit of the city's very first public water supply. Before Croton Aqueduct was built, the city's supply of fresh water from wells and springs was dwindling. Filthy water was a public health menace. The Aqueduct, completed in 1842, transformed city life. Water was piped down from upstate Croton River to reservoirs that are now the sites of Central Park's Great Lawn and NY Public Library's Bryant Park. A network of water mains then brought fresh water to homes and businesses.

Raised designs on early manhole covers gave horses better traction and pedestrians a handy way to scrape manure and mud from their boots. The city foundries took great pride in creating marvelous ornamental covers. Glance down as you cross the streets – there's a fascinating gallery of cast-iron artistry beneath your feet! You'll see many different intricate patterns of stars, flowers, honeycombs, ships' wheels, chain links, hexagons, some even with glass inserts. To the delight of urban archaeologists and artists, many have been catalogued and photographed as the subject of art books.

Take time to appreciate these extraordinary circular lids that seal off city pipes, cables, tunnels, and critters – both real and imagined.

Address Jersey Street (between Mulberry and Crosby Street), New York 10012 | **Transit** Subway: Broadway-Lafayette St (B, D, F, M); Bleecker St (6); Prince St (N, R), Bus: M5, M15, M21, M103 | **Tip** The Lower East Side Tenement Museum gift shop sells a circular floor mat that's a life-size replica of a NYC manhole cover.

83__ The Old Synagogue
From Ellis Island to Eldridge Street

In the nineteenth century, Lower East Side streets teemed with horses, pushcarts, and struggling humanity. Immigrants from Italy, Russia, and Poland poured in, with big families squeezed into stifling tenement rooms barely large enough for a table, chair, and bed. Amid the squalor, houses of worship were safe havens and social hubs.

Eldridge Street Synagogue was one of the first to be built in America by Eastern European Jewish immigrants. With donations from well-to-do congregants and a mortgage – the ashes of the paid-up mortgage are in a display case – it opened in 1887.

Inside the ground-floor Eldridge Street Museum is a modest hall where a small congregation still meets for Friday night and Saturday prayer. Public tours begin there. Savvy guides describe historical details, like why the sanctuary's chandelier is hanging upside down (it made sense when adapting gaslights to electric light bulbs), share anecdotes, and answer questions. On view is a treasured ark – a cabinet where torah scrolls are kept – that's older than the building.

Upstairs on the main level, the pretty entry hall won't prepare you for what you'll see when the sanctuary doors open. It is resplendent! Its 50-foot-high starry ceiling, skylights, stained glass windows, brass chandeliers, balcony, and *trompe l'œil* marble surfaces were designed to transport tenement dwellers to a place both sublime and otherworldly. One can only imagine the delight this brought to world-weary worshipers, how they would have wanted as much time here as possible – to pray, socialize, and escape from the chaotic world outside.

Sealed off in the 1950s and neglected for three decades, the sanctuary was rediscovered in 1986 and given landmark status. Twenty years and $20-million later, the restored synagogue reopened in 2007. A neighborhood treasure, it hosts concerts, lectures, festivals, and family programs throughout the year.

Address 12 Eldridge Street (between Canal and Division Street), New York 10002, Phone +1 212.219.0302, www.eldridgestreet.org | **Transit** Subway: East Broadway (F); Grand St (B, D); Canal St (6), Bus: M 9, M 15, M 22, M 103 | **Hours** Sun –Thu 10am – 5pm, Fri 10am – 3pm, closed Saturdays, major national and Jewish holidays | **Tip** At Russ & Daughters (179 East Houston Street) get a classic NYC bagel & lox with a *schmear* of cream cheese. The Russ family has sold the finest smoked fish and old-world Jewish *appetizing* here since 1914.

84__Paley Center for Media
The shows must go on

Its home is a building designed by Philip Johnson and its heart is the fourth-floor library, a large, low-lit space, silent except for occasional bursts of laughter from people viewing funny stuff. A librarian greets and escorts you to a seat at one of 42 consoles. Put on the headset and you have free access to a vast electronic archive.

Listen to radio broadcasts from the 1920s. Watch old and new TV shows – everything from 1940s black-and-white 'teleplays' to previews for next season. The Center's permanent collection of over 160,000 programs spans eras and genres: sports, sitcoms, soaps, game shows, political speeches, spectacles, world news, westerns, talk shows, thrillers, documentaries, cartoons, commercials. Do you love Lucy? If you're crazy for Cosby, devoted to Dr. Who, wild for Walter Cronkite, spellbound by Sopranos, you'll find your favorite episodes or one you missed. A click of the mouse and witness coronations, catastrophes, and Olympian record-setters. Hear Pavarotti sing, see Nureyev dance.

A 200-seat theater on the lower level hosts major screenings, seminars, and special events. Each event is recorded and catalogued, available to all interested in viewing its content. There's a second-floor theater as well as a more intimate screening room that school groups and fan clubs – admirers of specific shows – can reserve for hours of episodic delight.

Founded in 1975 by radio and television visionary William S. Paley, the Center (originally the Museum of Television and Radio) collects and preserves broadcast media, makes it accessible to the public, and contemplates its historical significance, impact on society, and artistic expression. A mecca for scholars from around the world, it's also a wonderland for artists and creators of traditional and emerging media.

Come to be entertained and revive childhood memories. The Paley Center is the best show-and-tell in town!

Address 25 West 52nd Street (between Fifth Avenue and Avenue of the Americas), New York 10019, Phone +1 212.621.6800, www.paleycenter.org, info@paleycenter.org | Transit Subway: 5 Av-53 St (E, M); 47–50 St-Rockefeller Ctr (B, D, F, M); 51 St (6); 50 St (1); 57 St-7 Av (N, Q, R), Bus: M1, M2, M3, M4, M5, M7, M20, M31, M50, M57 | Hours Wed and Fri-Sun noon–6pm, Thu noon–8pm | Tip Wine and dine next door at the legendary 21 Club, once a Prohibition-era speakeasy, and favorite hangout for celebs and VIPs.

85__The Panorama of NYC
The not-so-big apple

Feast your eyes on a giant 3-D model of the entire City of New York, laid out before you in one room! Every house, office tower, park, bridge, street, waterway. Stroll its perimeter along glass balconies and ramps overlooking spectacular aerial views of all five boroughs. You'll search out the familiar (for locals: your old school!) and the famous (Central Park!). Hard to imagine, but it's all there! A marvel and magnet for visitors, and a source of inspiration for artists and writers.

The Panorama – crown jewel of the NYC Pavilion in the 1964-65 NY World's Fair – was the brainchild of urban planning wizard Robert Moses, the Fair's president. In this exquisitely detailed scale model (one inch = one hundred feet), the Empire State Building stands fifteen inches tall, the Statue of Liberty less than two inches. For three years, a team of a hundred architects and model makers studied aerial photos and archival maps, handcrafting every tiny structure from bits of foam, wood, plastic, paperboard, and metal (for bridges). World's Fair visitors viewed the model from electric cars designed to simulate the experience of seeing it from a helicopter at 20,000 feet, with special lighting effects changing day into night.

In 1992, a massive expansion project transformed the former NYC Pavilion into what is now the Queens Museum. The Panorama was disassembled into 273 sections for renovation and updates, replacing 60,000 buildings. The new contemporary art museum opened in 2013 in a space twice its former size, with bright, spacious galleries, a dramatic glass wall facing the '64 Fair's iconic Unisphere, and its proud centerpiece – the reassembled, ever-fabulous Panorama.

Don't miss the museum's display of nostalgic artifacts from both the '39 and '64 World's Fairs, or the exceptional collection of Tiffany glass. Nibble a snack at the cafe, then snap a panoramic selfie in front of the Unisphere.

Address Queens Museum, Flushing Meadows-Corona Park, Queens, New York 11368, Phone +1 718.592.9700, www.queensmuseum.org, info@queensmuseum.org | **Transit** Subway: Mets-Willets Point (7) | **Hours** Wed – Sun noon – 6pm | **Tip** Ride one more stop on the #7 train to Main Street, Flushing – one of the largest Chinatowns outside of Asia – for an authentic taste of the Far East.

86__ The Park Avenue Armory

Building excitement

Occupying an entire block of the Upper East Side's most exclusive real estate is a brick fortress built in 1880. It was the headquarters for New York's National Guard 7th Regiment Militia, a hometown unit known as the 'Silk Stocking Militia' because most of its members hailed from the city's social elite. Gilded Age families that included Vanderbilts, Roosevelts, and Harrimans privately funded its construction, commissioning the same top-tier architects and interior designers who built and decorated their opulent city mansions and country palaces. Its drill hall – a 55,000-square-foot unobstructed space for military parades, musicales, and fancy dress balls – was a marvel of engineering. And no expense was spared in creating its elaborately adorned reception and regimental rooms to showcase the finest work of interior design artists like Louis Comfort Tiffany.

No matter when you visit, there's lots to see and do. Annual international art and antiques shows have called the Armory home for decades. Wander through or schedule a docent tour of the entrance, stairways, and historic period rooms, described by the NYC Landmarks Commission as "the single most important collection of nineteenth-century interiors to survive intact in one building." A $200-million restoration project is now reviving its original splendor.

Most exciting is the reimagining of the Armory as a cultural institution *par excellence*. Since 2007 the vast column-free drill hall has undergone countless reconfigurations to become a daring and unconventional venue for staging monumental masterpieces of international theater, music, dance, and visual art. The Royal Shakespeare Company actually rebuilt a full-size replica of their British theater inside the hall! Dynamic performance schedules and the Artists-in-Residence program ensure a vibrant future for the Armory – and thrilling experiences for contemporary audiences.

Address 643 Park Avenue (between East 66th and 67th Street), New York 10065, Phone +1 212.616.3930, www.armoryonpark.org | Transit Subway: 68 St-Hunter College (6); Lexington Av-63 St (F), Bus: M 66, M 101, M 102, M 103 | Hours Open during public hours of Armory programs. Check website. | Tip Asia Society Museum is nearby at Park Avenue & 70th Street. It has a lovely cafe, perfect for lunch or afternoon tea, and an enthralling gift shop.

87 Pastrami Queen

Love at first bite

It is said that you never forget your first love. And once you've tasted authentic New York pastrami you'll never forget your first bite. You know greatness when you taste it. Just the thought of it could make you stop whatever you're doing and fixate on the sheer sensual delight of a mouthful of tender, smoky, aromatic meat laced with garlic and crushed peppercorns. Exquisite fatty and lean slices piled high on fragrant rye bread. *Ooooh!*

A sandwich that was once available at every corner deli in Jewish neighborhoods on Manhattan's Lower East Side, in Brooklyn and the Bronx, *classic* New York pastrami is now increasingly hard to find. Out-of-towners generally consider all New York pastrami to be excellent since it's far superior to the processed meat-stuff bearing that name that's sold everywhere else. So while it's easy for New York delis to claim they're the best (and a select group of well-known delis do serve very good pastrami), seasoned New Yorkers can taste the difference and agree that Pastrami Queen really nails it.

It's a nondescript kosher-deli storefront on the Upper East Side, with a brightly lit counter and five tables that seat just sixteen patrons. It's small and it's not pretty, but the menu is expansive and seductive. Stand at the counter and watch the pros deftly slice your order of incomparable pastrami, or other deli delights – corned beef, brisket, tongue, turkey, roast beef, chicken, and chopped liver. They have luscious salads and sides, plus traditional kasha, knishes, potato pancakes, and matzo ball soup; crispy hand-cut fries, franks, and knockwurst. You can phone in an order for local delivery, stop by for take-out, or have Pastrami Queen cater your party.

But at least once, arrive early and sit at a table. In a flash, the waiter brings pickles and your hot pastrami sandwich. Grab it with both hands and prepare to fall in love.

Address 1125 Lexington Avenue (between East 78th and 79th Street), New York 10075, Phone +1 212.734.1500, www.pastramiqueen.com | **Transit** Subway: 77 St (6), Bus: M 1, M 2, M 3, M 4, M 15, M 72, M 79, M 101, M 102, M 103 | **Hours** Daily 10am–10pm | **Tip** The lower level of exquisite St. Jean Baptiste Church on 76th St & Lexington is home to the DiCapo Opera Theater, a "mini-Met."

88__PDT Speakeasy

Beyond the telephone booth

In the days of Prohibition (1920-33), a speakeasy was an illegal booze bar hidden in an unlikely spot behind a heavy door, its location – and often a secret password – known only to a select few. PDT (short for Please Don't Tell) is one such well-hidden gem. Although the address is on St. Marks Place, no matter how carefully you search, you won't find its front door. You enter through a hot-dog joint – Crif Dogs – under an eye-catching wiener-shaped sign with *"eat me"* mustard-scrawled on it. Discreetly step inside a vintage telephone booth, follow instructions posted on the wall, then dial a number on a rotary phone to reach the hostess.

A cool, intimate, cocktail lounge, PDT seats 45 patrons – no standees allowed – at an elegantly appointed rectangular bar and four oval booths. Oil paintings and stuffed critters (bear, otter, jackalope) adorn the walls. Virtuoso mixologists cheerfully concoct creative and classic specialty cocktails, made with high-end (and often rare) spirits and fresh ingredients, hand-crafted syrups, a variety of bitters – serving them with great panache. On-the-rocks drinks are chilled with a single giant cube that cools your libation but won't dilute it. If you crave a snack, order a Crif Dogs frankfurter with unexpected toppings like avocado, cream cheese, jalapenos, chili, bacon, pineapple, peanut butter. Add a side dish of waffle fries or ever-popular tater tots. Food is delivered via a small pass-thru at the mirrored back bar.

To ensure a warm welcome (and coveted seats), call ahead. Reservations are same-day only – the phone line is open from 3pm until they're fully booked. Weekend walk-ins should expect a lengthy wait: the hostess takes your name, then calls your mobile when seats become available. If you hate to wait, get there at 6pm on a weekday night when it's usually less busy.

Memories are made beyond the door of this hot-dog shop's phone booth.

Address Inside Crif Dogs, 113 St. Marks Place (between First Avenue and Avenue A), New York 10009, Phone +1 212.614.0386, www.pdtnyc.com | **Transit** Subway: Astor Pl (6); 1 Av (L), Bus: M 8, M 14, M 15, M 101, M 102, M 103 | **Hours** Mon – Fri 6pm – 2am, Sat – Sun 6pm – 4am | **Tip** Catch a play, dance performance, or reading at historic Theatre 80 (80 St. Marks Place), a former speakeasy, celeb-hangout jazz club, and art film house.

89__Rats on the Ropes
Odd facade of the Graybar Building

Most New Yorkers have encountered the beady-eyed stare of a big grey rat scurrying along subway tracks or hastily scavenging through a curbside pile of trash bags. These rodents live among us, thrive on refuse, carry disease, and multiply like crazy. A recent official report estimating that roughly two million rats currently reside in NYC was greeted with widespread skepticism. Streetwise city residents reckon the rat population more likely approaches the number of humans living here.

Rush hour commuters hurry in and out of Grand Central Terminal's Lexington Avenue entrance, rarely glancing above street level. But – stop, look up, and you'll see three rats climbing the poles supporting the rain canopy of the station's next-door neighbor, the Graybar Building. These three poles were designed to resemble a ship's mooring ropes. A cast-iron rat stands poised on each rope, facing a cone-shaped rat-guard preventing it from climbing any further. Take a closer look at the building's facade and you'll notice rosettes – not floral motifs, but circles of carved rat heads peering outward, as if gazing from inside a ship's porthole.

When it opened in 1927, the Graybar was the world's largest office building. While it was not the tallest skyscraper, it contained more square footage of office space than any other structure in the world, accommodating 12,000 workers, the population of a small city. The Graybar Company was an electrical merchandising firm, so it's curious the architects chose to put maritime imagery and rodent figures in the design. Perhaps it was to glorify NY's history as a vital seaport and distinguish it from neighboring Grand Central Terminal, a massive railway hub.

Years later, one rat mysteriously vanished. And while a restoration in 2000 replaced him with another, fans of this architectural oddity prefer to believe the missing critter finally scampered aboard the ship.

Address 420 Lexington Avenue (between East 43rd and 44th Street), New York 10170 | Transit Subway: Grand Central-42 St (4, 5, 6, 7, S), Bus: M1, M2, M3, M4, M42, M101, M102, M103 | Tip You won't find any rats at the Apple Store inside Grand Central Terminal but they sell a fine assortment of wireless mice.

90__Red Hook Winery
Fermenting a great idea

Inside an 1850s waterfront warehouse, alongside coffee roasters and pie makers, is a winery that makes a hundred different handcrafted wines. Improbable? Well, Brooklynite Mark Snyder challenged his two friends, fabled Napa winemakers Abe Schoener and Robert Foley, to create fine wine from New York-grown grapes. Accepting the challenge – and producing exceptional product – they launched Red Hook Winery.

Grapes harvested at fifteen different vineyards from upstate Seneca Lake and downstate Long Island are delivered by truck. Once they arrive, no time is lost. Stems and leaves removed, they're crushed by machine (some are stomped!), fermented in steel tanks, and aged in oak barrels imported from France (some costing as much as $3,000). Then, after two years, bottled. Every lot of grapes is split between the two winemakers, Schoener and Foley each developing half. The results get picturesque names like Joe's Tears Red Wine and One Woman Vineyard Sauvignon Blanc.

Come sample the wines at daily tastings. Order by the glass, then buy a bottle or case of any that sing to you. The rustic space is welcoming, evoking the tasting rooms of California wine country. A staff of young experts is eager to chat, explore your preferences, and help select from favorite varieties or suggest an especially excellent vintage. When you sample a wine you'd like to know better, order a glassful and chill out in the lounge area with fellow oenophiles.

Hurricane Sandy devastated the winery in October 2012. Nearly ninety percent of its inventory was lost when rising waters flooded the building, carrying off precious barrels and destroying equipment. An outpouring of community support in the storm's aftermath fueled a massive cleanup and rebuilding project. Six months later it reopened. Glasses were raised as great New York wine flowed once more in Brooklyn's hip Red Hook, letting the juice tell the story!

Address 175–204 Van Dyke Street, Pier 41–325A, Brooklyn, New York 11231, Phone +1 347.689.2432, www.redhookwinery.com, info@redhookwinery.com | **Transit** Subway: Smith-9 St (F, G), then Bus: B 57, B 61; or Ikea Ferry at Pier 11 at Wall Street to Fairway Market stop | **Hours** Mon – Sat 11am – 5pm, Sun noon – 5pm | **Tip** Try a "swingle" – sweet & tart chocolate-dipped frozen key lime pie at nearby Steve's Authentic Key Lime Pies.

91 Romantic Viewpoint

Enchanting esplanade along the river

High above the East River at the edge of a leafy-green neighborhood of townhouses and brownstones is one of the most romantic walkways in the city, a favorite spot for many New Yorkers – and it's in Brooklyn.

For good reason, the Brooklyn Heights Promenade has been featured in films like *Annie Hall* and *Moonstruck*. Whether you take a leisurely stroll or park yourself on a bench along its 1/3-mile-long esplanade, you'll be treated to picture-postcard views of the Statue of Liberty, Freedom Tower, lower Manhattan's skyline, and Brooklyn Bridge. On a scale of one to ten, the view from here is eleven. What you see in daytime – regardless of season or weather – is dramatic. But at dusk it's sheer magic. As the sun descends, the city is illuminated from behind, haloed in shades of pink, purple, and orange. When darkness falls, a-million-and-one lights blink on. It's a sight you'll treasure forever.

Brooklyn Heights is the oldest residential neighborhood in Brooklyn and its first Historic Preservation District. As early as the 1700s, rich merchants and sea captains built mansions here to enjoy its city and river views. Since colonial times, prominent New Yorkers have resided here, and many do now. The luckiest ones have windows that face the ever-changing skyline.

The Promenade, built in 1950 on an elevated platform, was designed to eclipse a major highway – the Brooklyn-Queens Expressway – connecting the adjoining boroughs. Hiding the busy traffic lanes beneath helps preserve the charm of the neighborhood.

This expanse of walkways, flowerbeds, play areas, and benches is ideal for strolling, jogging, sunbathing, reading, picnicking, and walking the dog. It inspires romance. Countless first dates here have led to marriage proposals on a return trip. There's no more perfect spot for a memorable photo or to strike up a conversation with fascinating folks from Brooklyn and the world beyond.

Address Columbia Heights between Joralemon Street and Grace Court, Brooklyn, New York 11201, Phone +1 718.965.8900, http://nyharborparks.org/ | **Transit** Subway: Clark St (2, 3); High St (A, C); Court St (R), Bus: B 25, B 26, B 38, B 41, B 45, B 52, B 61, B 63, NY WaterTaxi: Dumbo-Brooklyn Bridge Park | **Hours** Daily dawn–1am | **Tip** Brooklyn Historical Society is 3 blocks away at 128 Pierrepont Street. The landmark Queen Anne-style building dates back to 1881.

92___The Russian-Turkish Baths
Rub-a-dub-dub

If you're looking for a New Age health spa, this is not the place for you. Don't expect to be greeted by an aroma of sandalwood or the sound of wind chimes. The atmosphere at the Russian-Turkish Baths is far from ethereal and the staff is usually all-business, so most of the time you won't be greeted at all. This authentic, no-frills, nineteenth-century bathhouse (established 1892) is where Eastern European immigrants came to unwind after long, arduous workdays – to have a *schvitz* (sweat) to remove city grit and grime, slough off the cares of daily life, schmooze with *landsmen* (countrymen) in the steam room, and chew over hot topics and stuffed cabbage in the cafe.

The old spa is still in its original tenement building in a part of the East Village that was once a Ukrainian enclave. Despite interior renovations, upgraded facilities, and a diverse clientele – a crazy-quilt of old-timers and young hipsters – the bathhouse is essentially unchanged. It retains a heavy Russian accent, and it takes itself seriously. *Da,* you will leave feeling cleansed and renewed.

Once inside, exchange your clothes and shoes for a bathrobe and slippers, grab a towel and head to the baths, steam room, or massage area. Steam and sauna are punctuated by a dip in a bracingly cold pool. There are separate locker rooms for men and women; while the schedule includes a few women-only and men-only sessions, most of the time it's coed. "Like at the beach," says co-owner Boris.

Reservations not required. Walk-ins are welcome and member-ships are available. Rub downs (Swedish, deep-tissue, or sports massage) and special extras (fragrant oak-twig *platza*, Dead Sea mud exfoliation, or seaweed scrub) are also offered. Prices, compared with uptown spas, are quite reasonable.

The cafe serves basic homemade Slavic dishes – *borscht*, sausage, dumplings. And like the baths, the traditional food is definitely old-world and hearty.

Address 268 East 10th Street (between First Avenue and Avenue A), New York 10009, Phone +1 212.674.9250, www.russianturkishbaths.com, russianturkishbaths@gmail.com | **Transit** Subway: 1 Av (L); Astor Pl (6); 8 St-NYU (N, R), Bus: M 1, M 2, M 3, M 8, M 15, M 101, M 102, M 103 | **Hours** Open daily; check website or call for coed or men-only, women-only hours | **Tip** Veselka (144 Second Avenue) is open 24/7, serving Ukrainian comfort food like *pierogies*, *challah*, and *borscht*.

93 Scandinavia House

From gravlax to Garbo

This modern Park Avenue office building in Murray Hill holds an unexpected surprise – an impeccably designed, multi-level space that's the proud centerpiece of the New York headquarters of the American Scandinavian Foundation, whose mission is to celebrate vibrant Nordic culture. Scandinavia House offers an exciting and wide range of educational and arts experiences that make it a not-to-be-missed destination. For many New Yorkers of Danish, Finnish, Icelandic, Norwegian, and Swedish background, it's a vital and relevant connection to their heritage – and visitors from those countries flock there for a taste of home.

In 1911, Scandinavian-Americans created the foundation to serve their growing immigrant community. It was the first non-governmental international organization dedicated to "the development of goodwill through educational and cultural exchange," providing grants and fellowships to American and Scandinavian students, scholars, and artists. In 2000, it opened the doors to Scandinavia House – the jewel in its crown.

The variety of activities is bountiful, with something for all ages and interests. A schedule of daily and weekly events provides a picture-window on Nordic life, a veritable smorgasbord that includes film screenings, art and design exhibitions, concerts, lectures, family programs, storytelling, craft and educational workshops – even language classes. You'll marvel at the diverse choice of topics: the psychological impact of Edvard Munch's art, novelist Stieg Larson's tragic early demise, traditional Icelandic knitting techniques, Oscar contenders in foreign films.

Exquisitely designed clothing, jewelry, and decorative objects are to be found in the gift shop. And the adjacent Smorgas Chef restaurant offers a chance to dine on silky *gravlax* and Swedish meatballs with lingonberries, sipping wine or beer beneath the silvery branches of a birch tree. *Skol!*

Address 58 Park Avenue (between East 37th and 38th Street), New York 10016, **Phone** +1 212.879.9779, www.scandinaviahouse.org, info@amscan.org | **Transit** Subway: Grand Central-42 St (4, 5, 6, 7, S); 33 St (6), Bus: M 1, M 2, M 3, M 4, M 5, M 34, M 42, M 102, M 103 | **Hours** Mon – Sat 11am – 10pm, Sun 11am – 5pm (check website for gallery, library, and special events hours) | **Tip** Across Park Avenue is Church of Our Saviour, a Romanesque-style gem containing stunning carvings and statuary. Choral music at 11am Sunday mass is heavenly.

94__The Slave Galleries

A screaming silence

Climb the narrow, steep stairs and catch your breath. You're at the top of St. Augustine's Episcopal Church, inside a rare artifact of racial oppression called a slave gallery. African-American churchgoers were confined to this cramped garret (men in one space, women and children in another) hidden from view of the white congregation comfortably seated in pews below them. Sitting on its wooden floor, the enslaved, indentured, and free blacks could pray, sing, and gaze at the distant altar only through narrow windows in one wall.

It might surprise New Yorkers that during colonial times their city was the northern capital of the slave trade, with an enslaved population exceeding that of most cities in the South. Prominent citizens bought and sold African men, women, and children, and profited from their free labor. In 1827, New York outlawed this practice. Emancipation proceeded slowly, and the black population was still restricted and segregated.

St. Augustine's opened in 1828 as All Saints Free Church. Although slavery had been abolished a year earlier, it's likely these small top-floor galleries were designed to keep blacks segregated from – and unseen by – white worshipers.

St. Augustine's is now home to the largest congregation of African-Americans on the Lower East Side. For generations, its slave galleries were never mentioned. Few knew it existed. Nobody went up there.

Today the Slave Gallery Project is committed to the restoration and preservation of this 'sacred space.' Through recent collaboration with the Lower East Side Tenement Museum and an ongoing dialogue with religious and ethnic leaders, its mission to become a model for "museums of conscience" moves forward.

As with most African-American narratives, the story of slave galleries is an oral history. St. Augustine's is listening hard.

Address 290 Henry Street (between Montgomery and Jackson Street), New York 10002, Phone +1 646.312.7560, www.staugnyc.org, info@staugsproject.org | **Transit** Subway: East Broadway (F), Bus: M 9, M 14, M 15, M 21, M 22 | **Hours** By appointment, call to arrange a tour | **Tip** Nearby Bialystoker Synagogue was a stop along the Underground Railroad, a secret network that helped slaves escape to freedom.

95 Small Dog Run

Go to the dogs in Carl Schurz Park!

A promenade along the East River adjacent to verdant 15-acre Carl Schurz Park is home to a beloved oasis where Upper East Side residents and their furry companions mingle and play. Here, well-behaved little purebred pups are set free from the confines of city apartment life. Off-leash and exuberant, with tails wildly wagging, little pooches run circles around each other, race after tennis balls, leap, crouch, and pounce to the delight of their owners, and captivate anyone and everyone who strolls by.

Enter the riverfront promenade by walking east as far as you can on East 84th Street, past East End Avenue. Directly ahead is a breathtaking river view and a few steps away on the left is the small dog run: an immaculate and smooth-paved surface that's equipped with running water and drainage, doggie water bowls, pooper scoopers, poop disposal bags, and an occasional left-behind rubber squeak toy. A low fence with a secure gate encloses the modest-sized oval expanse.

Wooden benches line the inside of the fence where dog owners of all ages and descriptions mingle, while exchanging stories about Wookie's new groomer and neighborhood gossip. Benches on the promenade just outside of the fence provide convenient viewing stands for clusters of excited children who gather wide-eyed to observe the hilarious hijinks of chihuahuas, pomeranians, shih tzus, poodles, lhasa apsos, and assorted other miniatures.

Even though there's a lovely playground and lush, green, hilly Carl Schurz Park only steps away, you'll find it's a challenge to tear yourself away from the small dog run. Some locals insist it's better than the zoo. Take a small child or that book you've been meaning to read. You're likely to remain for quite a while. On the other hand, wise neighborhood insiders suggest you come alone, lose the book and socialize. Go to the dogs – it could be the beginning of a beautiful friendship.

Address East River Promenade (at East 84th Street between East End Avenue and East River), New York 10028, www.carlschurzparknyc.org | Transit Subway: 86 St (4, 5, 6), Bus: M 15, M 31, M 79, M 86 | Hours Daily dawn to dusk | Tip Meet, fall in love with, and take home your very own furry four-legged friend at the NYC ASPCA Pet Adoption Center (424 East 92nd Street).

96__Smorgasburg
Eat, drink, and be merry

You're invited to a foodie phenomenon on the Brooklyn riverfront. Ride the L train to the Bedford Avenue station and follow the procession of hungry hipsters to Smorgasburg. Make sure you come with an empty stomach, a pocketful of cash, and your Raybans.

Every Saturday from April to November, more than a hundred local and regional vendors assemble at a Williamsburg parking lot (also Sundays at Brooklyn Bridge Park) to create a food fest of incredible edibles from around the world that's sure to titillate your taste buds and tickle your imagination.

It's best to come before 1pm (it opens at 11am and popular items sell out early) and take a quick aisle-by-aisle tour to survey options before you commit. See what's on counters, cases, and grills; inhale intoxicating aromas; sample free tidbits. Notice the number of people standing in line at each stall and ask a few why they're willing to wait for that BBQ lobster roll. Seasoned New Yorkers know that the longest lines mean the yummiest food.

The variety of tasty choices and the roster of vendors are overwhelming. Young chefs incubate new culinary ideas here. Vegans, carnivores, even picky eaters can't resist gastronomic adventures – gobbling up Mexican corn *elote*, Belgian *frites*, Puerto Rican *mofongo*, *tostadas*, chocolate marshmallow cookie *s'mores*, *ramen* burgers, bacon-wrapped pretzels, fried anchovies, *macarons*, meringues, pickles, and popsicles. A large assortment of artisanal beverages, soft and alcoholic, helps wash it all down.

The Manhattan skyline view is terrific, but you'll spend more time people-watching. The crowd includes remarkably diverse individuals and Brooklynites in the latest hipster attire. There's an atmosphere of gleeful camaraderie.

Whether you sit at a table or bench, on the grass with a plateful of scrumptious morsels in your lap, or spend the day strolling and grazing, you'll have a delicious experience.

Address 90 Kent Avenue (between North 7th and 8th Street), Brooklyn, New York 11249, www.brooklynflea.com/markets/smorgasburg/ | Transit Subway: Bedford Av (L), Bus: B 32, B 62; East River Ferry: E 34th St, Manhattan to N. 6th St, Williamsburg | Hours Apr.–Nov. Sat 11am–6pm (rain or shine) | Tip Artists and Fleas is a nearby emporium overflowing with an eclectic mix of vintage and handmade jewelry, clothing, and art.

97 _ SoHo Sidewalk Surprise
Watch your step!

In the seventies, SoHo was the sizzling center of NY's art scene. Its huge industrial lofts and rock-bottom rents attracted artists hungry for studio/living space and also prestigious uptown galleries eager to exhibit large-scale works. As the district became hotter, trendy restaurants and boutiques proliferated and rents soared. Priced-out artists left for outer boroughs and galleries moved to Chelsea or the Lower East Side. Today, window-shopping has replaced gallery-hopping, but there's still cool art here. Edgy graffiti and bright murals adorn buildings, walls, and doorways – yet hardly anyone notices the surprising art hidden in plain sight, right beneath their feet!

All day long, bustling crowds tread on the sidewalk art that Ken Hiratsuka (aka Ken Rock) carved into the northwest corner of Broadway and Prince. Few are aware of it, though it's been there since 1984! The whimsical images are formed by one continuous line that never crosses itself, a style once described as "Keith Haring meets prehistoric petroglyph" (and sometimes is misidentified as Haring's). Rock, an admirer of guerrilla graffiti, decided to bring art to this corner, chipping away with hammer and chisel until the police chased him off. He returned sporadically, working an hour or two at a time – taking two years to complete the work.

Nearby, in front of 110 Greene Street, direct your eyes to the pavement to see Francoise Schein's 87-foot-long, 12-foot-wide *Subway Map Floating on a NY Sidewalk*. Stainless steel inlays embedded in the sidewalk trace the three main subway lines (as they were in 1986, when it was commissioned), with recessed lights representing stations. Funded by the building's owner, an art patron, it won that year's award for the city's best public-art project. Today, people walk right past it.

Next time you're in SoHo, tear your eyes away from the shop windows, shift your focus to the ground, and step onto art.

Address a) Ken Rock: Northwest corner of Broadway and Prince Street, New York 10012; b) Francoise Schein: 110 Greene Street (between Prince and Spring Street), New York 10012 | Transit Subway: Prince St (N, R); Broadway-Lafayette St (B, D, F, M); Spring St (6, C, E), Bus: M 5, M 21 | Tip Dominique Ansel Bakery (189 Spring Street) is home of the original Cronut, and many other mouthwatering pastry delights.

98__Stone Street

A taste of the high life

Meander through off-the-grid streets in the Financial District and you might stumble across a narrow cobblestoned two-block alleyway aptly named Stone Street that runs from the rear entrance of 85 Broad Street to Hanover Square. Quaint seventeenth-to-eighteenth-century Dutch and English houses along this tiny pedestrian-only street host an inviting array of taverns, pizzerias, cantinas, bistros, and patisseries. At lunchtime and after work, investment wizards and savvy singles flee Wall Street's imposing glass and steel towers to meet, greet, eat, and raise a glass – or more – in this historic passageway.

The assortment of international cuisines and quaffs is so enjoyable it's no surprise brokers and bankers prefer to keep this hidden treasure to themselves. Nevertheless – and especially in warm weather when rows of canopied picnic tables fill its entire expanse – many city natives and adventurous visitors consider Stone Street a prized destination for tasty bites, strong libations, and for meeting friends and making new ones.

This cobblestone thoroughfare dating back to 1658, most visible in colder months when outdoor tables and benches are stowed, is said to be the first paved street in Manhattan. The Great Fire of 1835 destroyed most of its buildings along with much of the city below Wall Street. Rebuilt and flourishing for a time, over the years it became a rundown, unsavory area. Fast forward to the 1990s, when Harry Poulakakos, owner of Wall Street hangout *Harry's at Hanover Square*, opened new taverns and eateries there. That spurred renewed interest in the area and led to a restoration project so successful that in 1996 the tiny passage was designated an historic landmark district.

Celebrations abound, including Cinco de Mayo, Oktoberfest, and September's famous Oysterfest, Manhattan's largest outdoor oyster festival. Go and enjoy a taste of the high life on Stone Street!

Address Stone Street, between Hanover Square and Coenties Alley, NY 10004 | **Transit** Subway: Wall St (2, 3, 4, 5); Bowling Green (4, 5); Broad St (J, Z); Whitehall St (R), Bus: M5, M15, M20 | **Tip** Have your photo taken with the world-famous bronze *Wall Street Bull*. Believed to be a good luck charm, he's north of Bowling Green Park at Broadway and State Street.

99_Sugar House Window
Relic of a notorious prison

In the pedestrian zone behind One Police Plaza and the Municipal Building stands a low wall with a barred window. This bit of masonry bore witness to a horrific chapter in early NYC history – but it's hardly noticed by the thousands of municipal workers, attorneys, citizens, and tourists who walk past it every day. If you stop somebody and ask what it is, the answer will probably be a shrug, or a wild guess: *It's a sculpture, right?* Wrong!

New York was the only city occupied by British and Loyalist forces for the entire duration of the Revolutionary War (1776–1783), so it was deemed the most practical site to incarcerate prisoners of war: American patriots and sympathizers. The British seized churches, barns, homes, warehouses, and even ships – repurposing them as tribunals and military prisons. A shocking truth is that more than twice as many war deaths occurred inside these unsanitary, overcrowded detention houses and ships than on colonial battlefields.

The red brick window-wall behind Police Plaza is a remnant of the infamous Rhinelander Sugar House, a five-story refinery and warehouse that once stood at the corner of Rose and Duane Streets. Considered one of the most brutal of the British prisons, it was a living hell where patriots were starved, tortured, and died of smallpox, typhus, dysentery, and yellow fever. Prisoners would elbow their way through a crush of condemned men to reach a small portal, like the window of this wall fragment, for a glimpse of the outside world. There, from between the thick iron bars, they witnessed rampaging redcoats and wildfires raging through chaotic streets.

Although the Sugar House was razed in 1892, two of its original window fragments were kept intact (the other is in the Bronx, in Van Cortlandt Park). Ghastly and ghostly tales of the Revolutionary War heroes haunting these walls have also survived for more than two centuries.

Address In the pedestrian zone behind 1 Centre Street (at Chambers Street), New York 10007 | Transit Subway: Brooklyn Bridge-City Hall (4, 5, 6); Chambers St (J, Z, A, C); Park Pl (2, 3), Bus: M 5, M 9, M 15, M 22, M 103 | Tip Learn much more about NYC's notorious past at CityStore (1 Centre Street), filled with books, souvenirs, and mementos.

SUGAR HOUSE-PRISON WINDOW

This window was originally part of the five story Sugar House built in 1763 at the corner of Duane and Rose Streets and used by the British during the Revolutionary War as a prison for American Patriots. The Sugar House was demolished in 1892 and replaced by the Rhinelander Building incorporating this window into the facade as an historical artifact.

The Rhinelander Building was demolished in 1968 and the site is now occupied by Police Headquarters.

JOHN V. LINDSAY
MAYOR

100__ Transit System Art
Surprise – the subway's an art gallery!

New Yorkers escape traffic-clogged streets and squeeze into subway cars as they scurry to and from work. Countless visitors, tourists from all over, are seen studying subway maps to get around town. It's common knowledge: the subway is the best way to go from point A to point B. But by swiping your MetroCard you also enter a vast gallery of fine art!

Thanks to the Metropolitan Transit Authority's Arts & Design program, launched in the 1980s, our subway system contains one of the largest site-specific public art installations in the world. Most pieces are made of durable materials – glass, terracotta, mosaic, bronze. Over 300 works (including music, digital art, photography) beautify stations, and spark curiosity and conversation.

Harried riders often fail to notice the art, but it's impossible to miss Tom Otterness's *Life Underground* – quirky bronze figures populating platforms, stairways, and paths of the 14th St/8th Ave station. His cartoony characters silently try to engage or mock passersby, often making satirical commentary on greed, social status, and power. Hey, look at that tiny guy on a bench clutching his moneybag!

Pop Art master Roy Lichtenstein's striking 53-foot-long *Times Square Mural* is located on the mezzanine level of NYC's busiest station. More highlights not to miss are Faith Ringgold's *Flying Home Harlem Heroes and Heroines* (125th St, Manhattan); Kristin Jones/Andrew Ginzel's *Oculus* (Chambers St, Manhattan); Ik-Joong Kang's *Happy World* (Main St Flushing, Queens); Robert Wilson's *My Coney Island Baby* (Stillwell Ave, Brooklyn); Romare Bearden's *City of Light* (Westchester Sq, Bronx); and Bill Brand's zoetrope-like *Masstransiscope* that appears animated as you ride between De Kalb and Myrtle Aves in Brooklyn.

Check the website for locations (or use *Meridian* app for iPhone). Be adventurous. As you travel the subway, hunt for outstanding art in NYC's stupendous gallery.

Address a) Times Square Station, 42nd Street and Broadway, New York 10036, b) 14th Street/8th Avenue Station, New York 10011. For other specific locations: www.nycsubway.org/perl/artwork | **Hours** Most subway stations are open 24/7; call 511 for info | **Tip** The Transit Museum shop in Grand Central Terminal (42nd Street & Vanderbilt Avenue) sells posters and souvenirs featuring subway and station art.

101__Tudor City

Utopia, ten minutes from Times Square

There's a city within the city, built high on a granite cliff across the avenue from the United Nations. Tudor City, a neo-Gothic style neighborhood created in the late 1920's as an "urban utopia," was patterned on the idea of an idyllic English country manor. The largest residential project in the city at the time, Tudor City offered unique amenities designed to attract middle-class tenants who were increasingly inclined to flee the city for leafier boroughs and suburbs. On a hill that formerly housed tenements and shanties, developer Fred F. French demolished every building except the 1871 Presbyterian Church of the Covenant, an architectural landmark. He built a cloistered village complex of twelve residential apartment buildings, private greens, a miniaturized 18-hole golf course, tennis courts, public parks, shops, a hotel, and restaurants. It was designed so nearly all of the windows faced toward Manhattan's skyline and the courtyards and gardens to avoid views of the industrial riverside and the stench emanating from a slaughterhouse below the cliff on First Avenue.

Today, beneath the jazz-age neon glow of the rooftop TUDOR CITY sign, the towering buildings with names like Windsor, Woodstock, Prospect, Tudor, and The Manor are home to more than 5,000 residents. Many apartments have stunning midtown vistas that include the Empire State and Chrysler buildings. Tree-lined walks, parks, a garden, and a children's playground continue to provide a green refuge from city streets, in an enclave miraculously set apart from crowded sidewalks and traffic.

It's a bit tricky to find Tudor City – which is part of its charm, and provides the exclusivity its residents cherish. From Second Avenue: walk uphill on either 41st or 43rd Street, or mount one of two tall staircases at 42nd. From First Avenue: climb the steep curved steps at 42nd Street.

Your reward: a hidden gem awaits.

Address East 41st Street to East 43rd Street (between First and Second Avenue) | Transit Subway: Grand Central-42 St (S, 4, 5, 6, 7), Bus: M 15, M 42, M 101, M 102, M 103 | Tip An ideal spot for taking fabulous photos of the Empire State and Chrysler Buildings, Tudor City's proximity to the United Nations has an added bonus: an exciting variety of ethnic restaurants serves the UN's international workforce in the East 40s around First and Second Avenues.

102__Under the High Line
Top-level art from the ground up

One visit to the High Line and you'll know why people flock there. A brilliantly landscaped mile-and-a-half promenade on an abandoned elevated railway line spans the Meatpacking and Chelsea districts. Winding past tenements and old factories, you get incomparable river and skyline views from an unusual vantage point – third-story level. Amid plantings of indigenous shrubbery, grasses, and flowering weeds, contemporary art engages in a year-round dialogue with nature.

Get up close to art on surrounding buildings, like Ed Ruscha's massive *Honey I Twisted Through More Damn Traffic Today* and Charles Hewitt's *Urban Rattl*e sculpture. Thomas Vuille's (*aka* M. Chat) signature fat yellow cat grins mischievously at passersby, while Jordan Betten's flowing nude dances to the vibe of his swirling rooftop painting below.

Brand new buildings by superstar architects cluster around and above the promenade, while beneath it, garages, warehouses, boarded-up tenements, and dive bars share side streets with chic boutiques, quirky shops, top-chef eateries, and major art galleries. Gallery-hopping is fun, but outstanding works by international artists are also right out there on the street.

At 24th Street & Tenth Avenue, French artist JR and Jose Parlá of Cuba created a striking, larger-than-life image of an old woman, part of their *Wrinkles of the City, Havana* series – portraits of Cuban elders old enough to have weathered the Revolution. One block north is Brazilian artist Eduardo Kobra's towering mural based on Alfred Eisenstaedt's famous WWII victory-day photo, *Times Square Kiss*. The joyous couple radiates in a burst of color above a street-level cityscape right out of 1945, complete with trolley, old sedans, and men in fedoras.

New creations pop up all the time, beckoning from walls, sidewalks, windows. It's an ever-changing landscape – and isn't that just what you expect from New York?

Address Gansevoort to West 34th Street between Tenth and Twelfth Avenue, New York 10011 | **Transit** Subway: 8 Av (L); 14 St (A,C,E); 23 St (C, E); 34 St-Penn Station (A, C, E), Bus: M 11, M 14, M 23, M 34 | **Tip** Sip artisanal cocktails at sunset in the ultra-cool Standard Hotel rooftop bar (848 Washington Street) for dazzling views of the skyline, the High Line, Hudson River, and beyond.

103__Urban Squats and Gardens

Otherwise occupied

Since the 1980s, Alphabet City – Avenues A, B, C, D in the East Village – has been a creative hotbed, a scene of fierce struggle, gleeful anarchy, and grassroots activism. While outsiders familiar with the musical *Rent* (written by squatter Jonathan Larson) got a stylized taste of its *vie boheme*, community insiders recently founded the Museum of Reclaimed Urban Space (MoRUS) to bear witness to its complex history. Tours are led by local guides with firsthand knowledge of once-abandoned buildings and vacant lots taken over by struggling musicians and artists to grow food and flowers. In a spirit of camaraderie, squatters effected changes that impacted the neighborhood, the city, and beyond.

MoRUS guides take you inside real squats, spaces considered uninhabitable (no running water, electricity, or heat) – where, over the years, artists, musicians, and social activists scavenged materials and pooled their talent, skill, and energy to carve out acceptable abodes: Bullet Space, an artists' squat named for a brand of heroin and bullet holes in its boarded-up windows when squatters moved in; C Squat, musicians' living quarters now sharing space with the museum; Umbrella House, a former squat that morphed into a resident-owned model of green, sustainable housing.

On the tour you visit guerilla gardens where community residents and families raise fruit, vegetables, herbs, and flowers in environments that encourage skill-sharing and experimentation. Thirty-nine gardens thrive in this neighborhood, surely the greatest concentration in the city. Pleasant refuges from the gritty streets, these leafy spaces are also incubators for collaborative innovation in urban agriculture and vital rallying places for social action.

Thanks to many of Alphabet City's successful – and once-radical – initiatives, things like dedicated bike lanes, recycling, and green construction have been adopted citywide.

Address Museum of Reclaimed Urban Space (MoRUS), 155 Avenue C (at 10th Street), New York 10009, www.morusnyc.org, info@morusnyc.org | **Transit** Subway: 1 Av (L), Bus: M 8, M 9, M 14A, M 14D, M 21 | **Hours** Tue and Thu – Sun 11am – 7pm | **Tip** Tompkins Square Park, 1960s hippie hangout and scene of 1980s riots, hosts annual events: Halloween dog parade, Wigstock drag festival, and a Ginsberg *Howl* festival.

104__ Visible Storage at the Met

Hidden riches

There's a secret museum-within-a-museum at the Metropolitan. Although it's been open since 1988, the Luce Center for the Study of American Art is so little known that you may just be the only person there. It's worth the search: on the first floor, to the right of the American Wing's neo-classical facade, look for a glass-box elevator and take it to level M.

Once you find it, the sight is astonishing and impressive. Aisle after aisle of floor-to-ceiling illuminated showcases extend far into the distance in all directions, each enclosing a huge variety of American fine art and decorative objects. It's not an exhibit – it's the 'open storage' facility used by the museum's curators. Nearly every object in the American Wing collection that isn't displayed in the public galleries and period rooms is right here – paintings, sculpture, furniture, woodwork, clocks, silver, glassware, ceramics. The bulk of the American collection can be viewed in this area.

This dazzling maze contains close to 10,000 individual items, arranged by type, material, chronology, and form with each piece meticulously indexed, catalogued, and pictured in the collection's database. Touch-screen monitors at the end of most display cases provide quick reference to what's inside, while more detailed information on each object is easily accessible at computer terminals in comfortable lounge areas and at the main entrance. Search the term "candlestick" to see photos of every candlestick in the collection. Touch the photos to get more info and a map to help you navigate there for an up-close look.

And before you leave, don't miss what at first glance appears to be wallpaper at the entrance to the Luce Center. It's actually a collage of individual photos of everything in the collection!

Happy hunting!

Address 1000 Fifth Avenue (between East 80th and 84th Street), New York 10028,
Phone +1 212.535.7710, www.metmuseum.org | Transit Subway: 77 St (6); 86 St (4, 5, 6),
Bus: M1, M2, M3, M4, M5, M79, M86 | Hours Sun–Thu 10am–5:30pm, Fri–Sat
10am–9pm | Tip Rub elbows with galleristas and society types in the espresso bar at the
elegant Milanese cafe, Sant Ambroeus, on 78th Street & Madison Avenue.

105__Wave Hill

Tranquility on the Hudson

You might be surprised to learn that the Bronx is home to a 28-acre year-round pastoral oasis. Wave Hill, just north of the island of Manhattan, is an antidote to the daily chaos of city life. Here you can wile away a lazy afternoon reading poetry, dreaming dreams, or scheming schemes in a relaxing lawn chair, breathing sweet air. There might be a string quartet on the terrace, accompanied by the sound of children at play. Take in the glorious views of the Hudson River and the distant New Jersey Palisades.

Wave Hill was built as a country home in 1843. Over the years, a series of owners held, restored, and expanded the property. Before becoming a NYC public treasure in 1960, it was privately leased as a summer residence to some illustrious tenants, including Mark Twain and Arturo Toscanini. It's said that family summers there inspired young Teddy Roosevelt's lifelong love of nature. It is now listed in the National Register of Historic Places.

If you choose to interrupt your musings and explore, you can enjoy a great many sights and activities to empower your own connection to nature. Wander the winding wooded paths, stroll its lush gardens – some manicured, others wild – and greenhouses, terraces, and pergolas. If you feel energetic, ten acres of shaded woodland trails beckon. Or duck inside a greenhouse where succulents thrive in a tropical climate.

Elegant historic buildings, once individual country estates and now restored to their former glory, host a variety of exhibitions, educational programs, family workshops, and visual and performing arts events. Browse the gift shop's array of goodies, including Wave Hill's own popular lawn chair, originally designed in 1918. It's a bit pricey, but if you're handy (and thrifty), you can purchase a set of plans and build one yourself.

As you sample the cafe's delectable fare, either indoors or out, feed your senses – in the Bronx!

Address West 249th Street and Independence Avenue, Bronx, New York 10471, Phone +1 718.549.3200, www.wavehill.org | **Transit** Subway: W 242 St (1) then free shuttle (check website); Bus: from Manhattan: BXM 1, BXM 2; from Bronx: BX 1, BX 7, BX 9, BX 10, BX12; Rail: Metro-North from Grand Central to Riverdale Station | **Hours** Nov. 1– Mar. 14 Tue – Sun 9am – 4:30pm; Mar. 15 – Oct. 31 Tue – Sun 9am – 5:30pm | **Tip** Riverdale Waterfront Promenade and Fishing Site hugs the shore of the Hudson, just a few steps away from the Riverdale Metro-North rail station.

106__ The Wedding Garden
A photo op for the happy couple

They're called City Hall weddings, but Manhattan's civil weddings are actually conducted several blocks north, in the City Clerk's Office. Once a dingy, unwelcoming chamber, like most impersonal government offices where you'd stand in line for a driver's license, the Manhattan Marriage Bureau got a major facelift and expansion when Mayor Michael Bloomberg decided to transform NYC into a world-class wedding destination. The hospitable new ground-floor location has a spacious waiting area for people-watching, two inviting chapels for contemplation, and restrooms with full-length mirrors and a vanity table for spiffing up before you say "I do."

Over 20,000 couples get hitched by the City each year. At the City Clerk's Office, fill out all the requisite forms (also available online), get the marriage license, and then return – at least 24 hours later, and with a legal-age witness – to tie the knot in a friendly ceremony. You don't need to be a US citizen; just show your passport with the paperwork. NYC wedding-themed goodies and souvenirs are sold right on the premises at CityStore: fresh bouquets, garters, tiaras, faux diamond rings, rhinestone-studded bride & groom baseball caps (hers has a veil!), disposable cameras. And photographers hanging out on the sidewalk – your very own *paparazzi!* – offer their services to happy couples.

After exchanging vows, kisses, and congratulations, grab your Certificate of Marriage Registration and usher your new spouse across the street to the scenic Wedding Garden. Stroll past park benches of texting attorneys and clerks to this small garden area, just big enough for two, tucked into a dramatic backdrop of towering courthouse pillars. This lovely leafy bower, embraced by flowering shrubs and trees, provides a suitably romantic spot for smiling newlyweds to record their first married moments.

Then *click* to show how well you two click!

Address Wedding Garden: Southeast corner Centre and Worth Street, New York 10013;
Manhattan Marriage Bureau: 141 Worth Street (at Centre Street), New York 10013 |
Transit Subway: Brooklyn Bridge-City Hall (4, 5, 6); Chambers St (A, J, C); City Hall (R);
Canal St (N, Q), Bus: M 5, M 9, M 22, M 103 | Hours Wedding Garden: daily 6am – midnight;
Manhattan Marriage Bureau: Mon – Fri 8:30am – 3:45pm | Tip Celebrate love with a
champagne toast at Delmonico's (56 Beaver Street), America's first dining restaurant, a
landmark since 1837.

107__Weehawken Street

A shady lane with a shadowy past

Walk as far west as you can on Christopher Street, then look for tiny Weehawken Street. Manhattan's shortest one-block street is also one of its narrowest. Quiet, tree-lined, with only fourteen houses, this quaint lane appears in nineteenth-century etchings and drawings. An off-the-beaten-track enclave of jazz-age artists and writers, it's now a historic landmark. Today, the street's peaceful charm belies its colorful history.

Newgate Prison, NY's first state penitentiary, was on nearby Charles Lane. When it closed in the 1820s and its prisoners "sent up the river" – the origin of that phrase – to Sing Sing, further north on the Hudson, the city opened a public produce market. Farmers ferried fruits and vegetables from Weehawken, New Jersey, to sell at stalls in the tiny lane, lending the street its name. The market failed within a decade but its proximity to the Hudson docks made the street ideal for stables, maritime businesses, bawdy houses, and saloons. Many buildings faced the wharf, their main entrances on riverfront West Street and back doors on Weehawken.

The block's oldest structure is a wood-frame house – one of the few left in Manhattan – with a low, gabled roof and an unusual exterior staircase. It's probably a section of the original Weehawken Market House, an open-air shed with multiple stalls for merchants to display and peddle goods. Changing hands many times over the past two centuries, it's been a saloon, oyster house, gambling den, and pool hall – popular hangouts for longshoremen, haulers, and drifters. Weehawken and West Streets became a nucleus of tawdry, rough taverns. In the 1970s, West Street was a gritty strip of dockside gay 'leather bars' and sex clubs whose patrons rendezvoused in the shadows of Weehawken.

Its residences now command steep prices and are well-tended, but as you stroll its brief length, just imagine the tales this little lane might tell.

Address Between West 10th and Christopher Street (east of West Street and west of Washington Street), New York 10014 | **Transit** Subway: Christopher St-Sheridan Sq (1), Bus: M 5, M 8, M 11, M 20, M 21 | **Tip** See a pictorial mosaic of colonial Newgate Prison on the wall of the Christopher Street-Sheridan Square subway platform.

108 — The Whispering Gallery
Cool acoustic oddity

Pssst! We'll let you in on a little secret. There's an invisible communications system – a trick of sound-magic – hidden in plain sight right in busy, noisy Grand Central Terminal.

Go (with a friend!) to the terminal's dining concourse, outside the legendary Oyster Bar. As you face the wall in one corner of the ceramic-tiled arch where the two walkways intersect, speak softly into the wall. And in spite of the cacophony inside the vast, bustling train station, your friend facing the wall in the opposite corner will hear your words clearly, as if you were standing right beside her! This is the Whispering Gallery.

Unique physical properties of this spot are responsible for producing this amazing auditory phenomenon. The "Tile Arch System," a precise method for construction of arches and vaulted ceilings, was the invention of Spanish architect Rafael Guastavino, who patented it in 1885. Guastavino-tiled areas were constructed on this ramp of the terminal's lower level and also inside the Oyster Bar. Take a close look at these walls, arches, and domes. Observe the herringbone-pattern of the interlocking terracotta tiles and you'll notice how they flow smoothly along the curved surfaces. It's apparent that the special sound-reflecting ability of the Whispering Gallery is not accidental. The design was carefully calculated to focus and project sound across the dome to the opposite side.

Until you've actually tried it, you won't believe it works – and you won't forget that first time. It's so much fun! What you choose to say in hushed tones – and whom you choose to say it to – is strictly up to you.

Some reveal a secret, others sing a song. Lovers have proposed marriage there. And it's said that celebrated jazz musician Charles Mingus used to play his bass in one of its corners for maximum acoustic effect. How cool is that!

Address Grand Central Terminal, Dining Concourse, 87 East 42nd Street (between Lexington and Vanderbilt Avenue), New York 10017, www.grandcentralterminal.com | **Transit** Subway: Grand Central-42 St (S, 4, 5, 6, 7), Bus: M 1, M 2, M 3, M 4, M 5, M 42, M 101, M 102, M 103 | **Hours** Daily 5:30am – 2am | **Tip** Oyster Bar serves a great variety of fresh oysters and a seafood menu from each day's catch. The dining concourse offers many only-in-NY specialties and ethnic delights.

109 — White Horse Tavern

Manhattan's most haunted pub

Actor Charles Laughton played cribbage at the bar before this historic tavern became a watering hole for thirsty writers like James Baldwin, Anais Nin, Norman Mailer, and Allen Ginsberg. Jack Kerouac was thrown out so often, the words *Jack Go Home* were scrawled on the bathroom wall. Musicians Jim Morrison, Mary Travers (of Peter, Paul and Mary), and the Clancy Brothers downed countless pints here. A young Bob Dylan strummed his guitar and sang for tips.

The *original* Dylan, hard-drinking Welsh poet Dylan Thomas, is responsible for making the White Horse as infamous as it is famous. Thomas was a twice-daily regular who enjoyed its cheap libations and the easy camaraderie of fellow boozy literati, locals, and curious tourists who filled the barstools and tables of this popular hangout. One November night in 1953, the 39-year-old poet had his last drink here. After chugging eighteen shots of whiskey, he collapsed on the sidewalk, went into a coma at the Chelsea Hotel, then died at nearby St. Vincent's Hospital. The White Horse was Dylan Thomas' favorite haunt while he lived, and many believe that it's still true – insisting his ghost frequently drops by after closing time for a pint (or three) at the corner table beneath his portrait.

This authentic 1880 pub's proximity to the nearby Hudson River docks made it an early hangout of longshoremen. Before becoming a legendary literary lair, the White Horse was a haven for union organizers as well as the birthplace of the idea for the liberal *Village Voice* newspaper. Kitschy porcelain figures of white horses and other mementos decorate its walls and shelves. Drinks and pub grub remain cheap (cash only), and summertime sidewalk tables are perfect for leisurely people-watching. Visit on November 9th, the anniversary of Dylan Thomas' death, and order from the menu what is billed as his last meal there. Then drink a toast to the poet's ghost!

Address 567 Hudson Street (at West 11th Street), New York 10014, Phone +1 212.989.3956 |
Transit Subway: Christopher St-Sheridan Sq (1); 14 St (A, C, E, 2, 3); 8 Av (L),
Bus: M 8, M 11, M 12, M 14, M 20 | **Hours** Sun –Thu 11am – 2am, Fri – Sat 11am – 4am |
Tip Pub-hop across town to another historic tavern, one of the city's oldest: McSorley's,
established 1854. In 1970, women were finally admitted inside.

110_Winnie-the-Pooh
Friends forever – even longer

You may think he lives in The Hundred Acre Wood, but the real Winnie-the-Pooh is happily at home – with Kanga, Piglet, Eeyore, and Tigger – in the Children's Center at the main branch of the New York Public Library.

Years before his reinvention by the Disney animation studios, this chubby stuffed teddy bear belonged to a real British boy named Christopher Robin Milne. His father bought the bear at Harrod's of London in 1921 and gave it to him for his first birthday. Christopher called him Edward (the proper form of Teddy), but later changed that to Winnie, the name of a black bear at the London Zoo who was named after the city of Winnipeg, Canada.

Christopher's dad, playwright A. A. Milne, so enjoyed watching his son play with Winnie and his stuffed animal pals that he made up stories about them to tell the boy at bedtime. In these tales, a young lad named Christopher Robin had adventures with Winnie-the-Pooh and his friends in a forest that resembled the woods near the Milne's country house. As the stories grew longer, poems were added, and illustrator E.H. Shepard made drawings for what became four beloved books: *When We Were Very Young* (1924), *Winnie the Pooh* (1926), *Now We Are Six* (1927), and *The House at Pooh Corner* (1928). They were an instant sensation.

Beginning in 1947, when his stories reached the United States, the real Winnie toured throughout the country, frequently returning to England. In 1987, to the enormous delight of Americans and the outrage of many British, American publisher E. P. Dutton donated him to the New York Public Library. A member of Parliament tried to have him brought back to England – to no avail.

Pooh's adventures are translated into many languages and the endearing character has captured the hearts of children of all ages around the world. Visit Winnie and a 1926 photo of the real Christopher and his dad. If you can, do bring a pot of 'hunny.'

Address Children's Center at NY Public Library, Fifth Avenue at 42nd Street, New York 10018, Phone +1 917.275.6975, www.nypl.org | **Transit** Subway: 42 St-Bryant Park (B, D, F, M); 5 Av (7); Grand Central (4, 5, 6), Bus: M 1, M 2, M 3, M 4, M 5, M 7, M 42 | **Hours** Mon, Fri, Sat 10am–6pm, Tue, Wed 10am–7:30pm, Sun 1–5pm | **Tip** Over 15 million items reside in the NYPL main branch. All exhibits are free and as impressive as many in the museums. Visit the Map Room, Menu Collection, and a genuine Gutenberg Bible.

111 Yorkville's Glockenspiel

Where time stands still

When you first notice the antique mechanical clock at the corner of East 83rd and York, you wonder whether its horses will prance on the hour or half-hour, and if their motion will be accompanied by music-box melodies. Take a second look and you'll be astonished at what appears to be a wonderful old clock with movable figures – like those you'd see in old quarters of European cities. It's actually a flat mural painted on a wall! This is a contemporary example of *trompe l'oeil*, art designed to fool the eye.

The developer of a high-rise luxury condo on the opposite corner faced a problem – a graffiti-clad tenement across the street was an eyesore that would dominate the view seen from the lower floors of these pricey residences. He persuaded the tenement's owner to allow him to paint its exterior, and in 2005 hired acclaimed *trompe l'oeil* master Richard Haas to execute a 77-foot-wide mural of artistic trickery.

Paying tribute to Yorkville's long history as a German neighborhood, a glockenspiel became the focal point of Haas's work, an ancient clock incorporating delightful contemporary updates. Instead of traditional medieval knights on horseback circling the platform above the clock's inner works, he depicted the horsemen as NYC mounted police. The clock's face displays the twelve zodiac signs with a golden sunburst at its center. The internal mechanism is visible, detailing its wheels and gears. Faux imagery abounds: wacky gargoyles at street level, items inside windows, a curving interior stairway, and many architectural elements covering the facade are cleverly conceived and brilliantly executed. It looks so three-dimensional, so real, you'll want to touch it to prove to yourself that it isn't!

Yorkville families love to point out their glockenspiel, forever frozen at four o'clock. It's a bit of whimsy and an exciting landmark in their otherwise unsurprising residential community.

Address Northwest corner of East 83rd Street and York Avenue, New York 10028 |
Transit Subway: 86 St (4, 5, 6), Bus: M 15, M 31, M 79, M 86, M 101, M 102, M 103 |
Tip Schaller & Weber on Second Avenue and 86th Street has sold the best wurst since 1937, when Yorkville was known as Germantown.

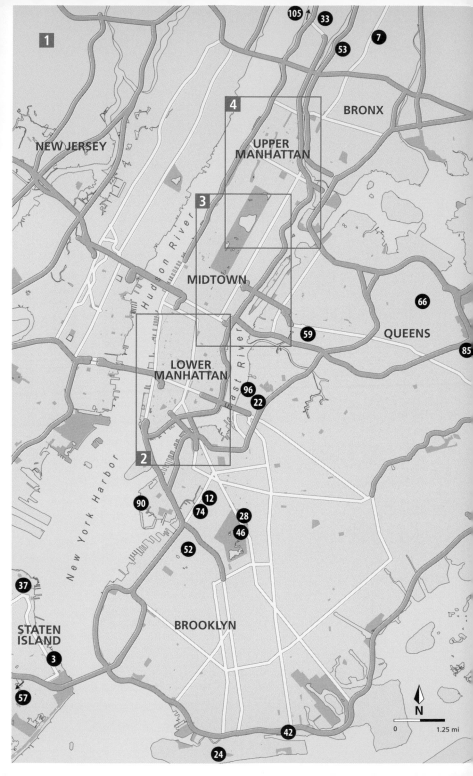

Desa Philadelphia
**111 SHOPS IN LOS ANGELES
THAT YOU MUST NOT MISS**
ISBN 978-3-95451-615-5

Gordon Streisand
**111 PLACES IN MIAMI AND THE
KEYS THAT YOU MUST NOT MISS**
ISBN 978-3-95451-644-5

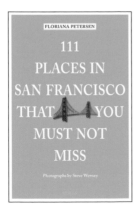

Floriana Petersen
**111 PLACES IN SAN FRANCISCO
THAT YOU MUST NOT MISS**
ISBN 978-3-95451-609-4

Sally Asher, Michael Murphy
**111 PLACES IN NEW ORLEANS
THAT YOU MUST NOT MISS**
ISBN 978-3-95451-645-2

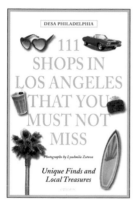

Desa Philadelphia
**111 SHOPS IN LOS ANGELES
THAT YOU MUST NOT MISS**
ISBN 978-3-95451-615-5

Kirstin von Glasow
**111 SHOPS IN LONDON THAT YOU
SHOULDN'T MISS**
ISBN 978-3-95451-341-3

Kirstin von Glasow
**111 COFFEESHOPS IN LONDON
THAT YOU MUST NOT MISS**
ISBN 978-3-95451-614-8

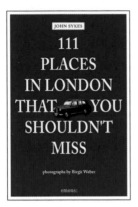

John Sykes
**111 PLACES IN LONDON THAT YOU
SHOULDN'T MISS**
ISBN 978-3-95451-346-8

Lucia Jay von Seldeneck, Carolin Huder,
Verena Eidel
**111 PLACES IN BERLIN THAT YOU
SHOULDN'T MISS**
ISBN 978-3-95451-208-9

Rüdiger Liedtke
111 PLACES IN MUNICH THAT YOU SHOULDN'T MISS
ISBN 978-3-95451-222-5

Peter Eickhoff
111 PLACES IN VIENNA THAT YOU SHOULDN'T MISS
ISBN 978-3-95451-206-5

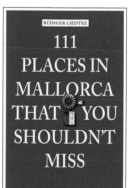

Rüdiger Liedtke
111 PLACES IN MALLORCA THAT YOU SHOULDN'T MISS
ISBN 978-3-95451-281-2

Acknowledgements

My sincere gratitude to Susan Lusk and Mark Gabor for bringing me onboard, for being brilliant editors and the best of friends; to the awesome team in Germany: Achim Mantscheff, Monika Elisa Schurr, Constanze Keutler, and Gerd Wiechcinski for meticulous work and great humor; to Gita Kumar Pandit for her Leica. To Mom, Jarrin kids and grandkids, my Komansky PICU family, Barads, and friends – thanks for your love and encouragement.

Author and Photographer

Jo-Anne Elikann was born in Brooklyn, grew up in Queens, and lives in Manhattan. The day her parents let her ride the subway she fell hopelessly in love with the city, and has feasted on its smorgasbord of extraordinary experiences ever since. A freelance writer, artist, and photographer whose proudest achievement has been raising six kids in a NYC apartment, her career includes stints as an art/antiques cataloguer, director of a children's art center, partner in a graphics firm, and healthcare administrator. She's a die-hard New Yorker and lifelong explorer of its nooks, crannies, and endless power to amaze.